Pleiadian Soul

"Humanity needs wisdom from higher perspectives at this critical time in our evolutionary journey. The description of the need for humanity's healing is essential in our world. Pavlina Klemm's *Pleiadian Soul Healing* is a wonderful and profound addition to Pleiadian wisdom that is being brought to humanity at this time. It is deep and meaningful knowledge. A must-read!"

— PIA ORLEANE, Ph.D., and CULLEN BAIRD SMITH, authors of
Pleiadian-Earth Energy Astrology, Remembering Who We Are,
and *Pleiadian Manual for Accelerated Evolution & Ascension*

"*Pleiadian Soul Healing* is a work of love. As Pleiadians said in the book, 'Everything is made of love.' The soul, mind, and body are one, and we have free will to live a fulfilling life. Pavlina Klemm and her Pleiadian guides share uplifting messages accompanied by practical guided exercises to liberate you from the past that has burdened you. Everyone has an innate ability to heal. With the counsel of Klemm's Pleiadian guides, you will be encouraged to tap into your own personal healing abilities and move forward into the life you desire."

— EVA MARQUEZ, author of *Activate Your Cosmic DNA*
and *Pleiadian Code*

PLEIADIAN
SOUL HEALING

LIGHT MESSAGES FOR COSMIC FREEDOM

Pavlina Klemm

Translated by
Hilary Snellgrove

 FINDHORN PRESS

Findhorn Press
One Park Street
Rochester, Vermont 05767
www.findhornpress.com

Text stock is SFI certified

Findhorn Press is a division of Inner Traditions International

Originally published in German by AMRA Verlag & Records as
Lichtbotschaften von den Plejaden 8: Im Feld der Heilung

Disclaimer
The information in this book is given in good faith and intended for information
only. Neither author nor publisher can be held liable by any person for any loss
or damage whatsoever which may arise from the use of this book or any of the
information therein.

Cataloging-in-Publication data for this title is available from the Library of Congress

ISBN 978-1-64411-829-0 (print)
ISBN 978-1-64411-830-6 (ebook)

Printed and bound in the United States by Lake Book Manufacturing, LLC
The text stock is SFI certified. The Sustainable Forestry Initiative® program
promotes sustainable forest management.

10 9 8 7 6 5 4 3 2 1

Edited by Nicky Leach
Cover and interior illustrations by Josephine Wall, www.josephinewall.co.uk
Text design and layout by Damian Keenan
This book was typeset in Adobe Garamond Pro, Calluna Sans, and with
ITC Century Std used as a display typeface.

To send correspondence to the author of this book, mail a first-class letter to the
author c/o Inner Traditions • Bear & Company, One Park Street, Rochester,
VT 05767, USA, and we will forward the communication, or contact the author
directly at **https://pavlina-klemm.com**

*I dedicate this book to all people of goodwill
who have come to this planet to illuminate
the reality of humankind through the power
of their heart's light.*

*I also dedicate it to all those people who have
come to this planet with the task of liberating the
reality of their earthly being and thus ascending
into higher dimensions of consciousness.*

*It is my wish that all human beings may find
their heart's light and their spiritual freedom
within themselves and inspire others.*

With love
Pavlina

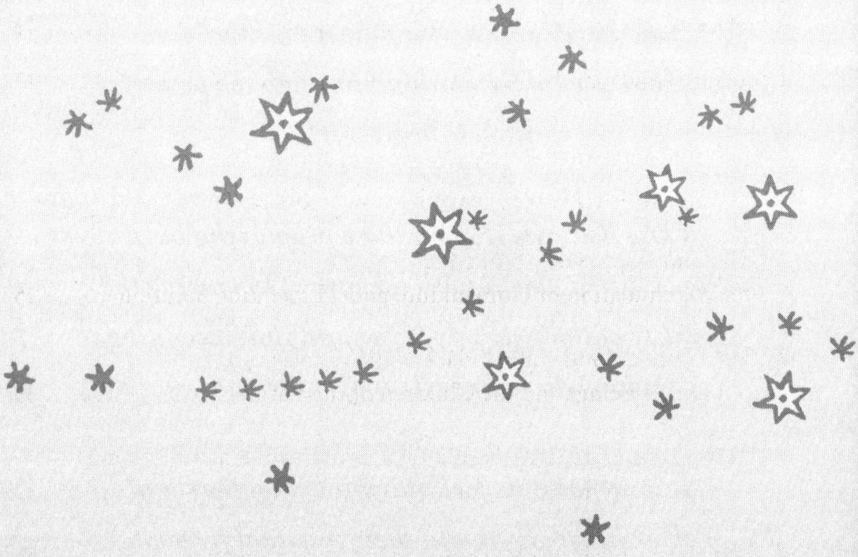

Contents

PART TWO
Messages from the Pleiadians

APPENDICES

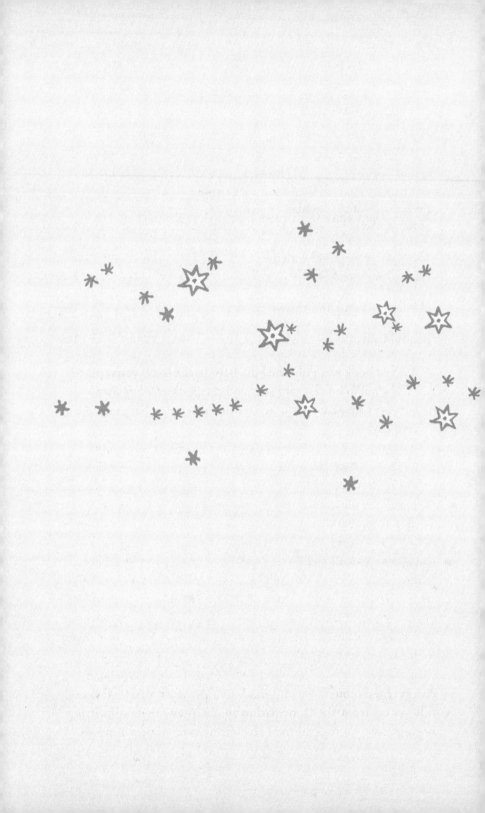

Preface

Dear reader of these light-filled messages!

In your hands, you are holding my eighth book in the series *Light Messages from the Pleiades*. I myself can hardly believe the speed with which the Pleiadian beings have transmitted so much information to me, and that, thanks to them, eight books with these light-filled messages have now been written.

The first book was published in 2016. In the last 8 years, practice CDs, audio books, card sets, and the book *Healing Symbols & Number Sequences*, published outside this series, have seen the light of day.

The Pleiadians accompany us on our path and convey countless pieces of information to enable us to help ourselves as best we can, so that we can recognize the light in our soul and determine what is essential in life and existence.

They accompany us, as they themselves say, step by step, and deliver the information in such a way that, in its entirety, it is suitable for us and can be received. They convey information so that we are able to understand the overall picture and understand that each one of us influences our environment and that our environment influences us.

The law of action and reaction is one of the laws that is revealing itself to us more than ever before.

In these eight volumes, each individual book has a specific energy. Even though the information in the texts presented here follows on from the information in the previous books, it is not necessary to read all the books from the first one onwards, certainly not in the order in which they appeared. People often ask me which book they should start with, and I always give them the answer that the Pleiadians gave to me:

"Feel into the energy of the individual books, or look at the covers of the books. The book that particularly attracts you is the one that your soul desires and whose energy and light information your soul needs right now."

Each book carries its very own energy, its own information, and the words in these books are energetically programmed so that the soul and consciousness of the reader can decipher these "keys" and the overall system of the human being can become healthy.

It is possible to read the books individually, although the book texts build on each other, because the information they carry has always been transmitted in such a way that the themes within each book are rounded off, and the information in the individual books makes sense even if preceding books are left out.

And that is what is so fascinating about the information in these books. They can be read individually, and yet they build on each other.

The information that the Pleiadians convey to us goes into even more depth with each further book written, and the scope of the content also increases. And yet, the Pleiadians still manage to include current situations, as well as those from the past and future of humanity, and to simultaneously transfer information on how to heal the varied systems in our body, soul, and mind as well as in our society.

With each text I received from the Pleiadians, I kept thinking how incredibly thoughtful, wise, and fascinating these texts are. What I also find fascinating is that their texts are charged with positive, loving energy. Even if some information concerning our earthly presence is not particularly pleasant, they always offer us a variety of solutions for each particular situation mentioned and transmit to us the energy of motivation. This helps us to find more strength within ourselves than ever before and to move forward with confidence.

The Pleiadians move and exist in a time–space different from that of our human community. More precisely, from our perspective, they live in the future; therefore, they can look back on our present and convey information about things that will help us on our way and will occur in our future. They connect with us in our entirety and then gauge which phase of consciousness we are in and which information is suitable to be passed on to us. In the process, we retain free choice and free will at all times.

All of us, including the Pleiadians, wish, of course, for as many human beings as possible to choose a positive, light-filled future—the one that has already been programmed for us by Divine Intelligence.

The Pleiadians are near me at all times and communicate the information for the books and messages to me with the help of telepathic and visual transmission. For every piece of information I write down, I receive additional visions, images, and colors to enable me to understand the meaning of this information as clearly as possible.

I also feel their emotions—the love, compassion, and gratitude of the Pleiadians. While writing, I often felt their concern as to whether we will really choose a positive future. I often have felt their concern for all of us who face the challenges of earthly life, every day, because, as we all know, our plans, when we made them in the realms of the heaven of human beings, felt different then to how they feel now—in the human body, in this reality, here on Earth.

Each book in the *Light Messages from the Pleiades* series is located in its own morphogenetic fields, which the Pleiadians have programmed and to which I have access. In each case, I am able to feel if the contents of the book are already complete and if I can start writing and "downloading."

In this book, the one that you are about to begin reading, we have been greatly honored. The individual members of the Pleiadian group communicating with me introduced themselves by name and shared some information about themselves. Beginning with this book, dear readers, you will know specifically who is communicating with you, who is transmitting energy to you, who is programming the number sequence, and who is responsible for transmitting information for our healing and for the state of our planet.

Everything is becoming more and more concrete. I think this is because a large number of people are already working with these books, and that this has given the Pleiadians the opportunity, and the possibility, to make specific and personal contact with those who are ready for their growth in consciousness and the healing of their personal system.

Each book written further enables us to feel how much the Pleiadians love us, and how much they want the transition to a positive future to succeed and take place without unnecessary losses. Their tireless help is tremendous.

While writing down their information, I was often struck by the enormous patience they have with us human beings. We keep falling back into our old, negative habits and well-worn paths—and they carry on helping us to get back up and keep moving forward. I appreciate their help very much. I appreciate every piece of information and all the loving energy they give us.

I also truly appreciate the energy transmissions they undertake with us every Monday. Every Monday between 21:00 and 21:20, local time, they work with anyone who chooses to develop their consciousness and heal themselves. From experience and through feedback from advocates of Pleiadian healing energies, I can confirm that thousands of people are now participating in these transmissions. I know that my readers and the advocates of the Pleiadian energies are at home all over this world.

Anyone who connects with the Pleiadians and their radiant, healing energies at 21:00 in their respective local time is increasing not only their own light but the light of the entire population of Earth and the light of the entire planet.

Pleiadians often say that the human community is like a living organism. We mutually influence each other; that is, every one of us influences everyone else, even if we are not aware of it. The law of action and reaction as well as the law of resonance work perfectly—now more than ever before.

At this time, with the increase in the planet's light vibration and with a huge amount of cosmic light streaming toward us, we can use our positive power not only for our own growth and healing but also for the growth and healing of the whole.

Like a living organism, we receive the frequencies of the cosmos; that is, we receive the love and the light of the cosmos and the life-giving energy of the earth. Every day, as in any living organism, individual cells die, and every day, new cells are born or formed. A new luminous structure is emerging. Humanity, just like any other positive organism, longs for life-giving energy, for light and for love.

It is to these divine magnitudes—light and love—that we aspire: At first, as individuals, everyone for themselves, as we have done for a long time (it not having been possible to do otherwise until now), but in the near future that will change, as long as we connect and strive together. We will walk hand in hand, because we will feel that our connectedness gives us much more strength, energy, and motivation than if we walk alone on this path to the light.

We will feel the positive power of the collective as that state in which we once lived and that enriched us. We will feel that a healthy organism can only function if each one of us takes on a particular task, one we like doing and that feels natural to us. And this very task will not only have a positive effect on us; it will have a positive effect on the whole.

We are in a phase of discovering and recognizing new possibilities. What has served us for years no longer serves us now, because the energies of certain structures and systems no longer carry enough power and vigor. Many structures and habits will disappear. They are virtually disintegrating by themselves, because the energy that used to nourish them no longer exists on Earth.

And many low-frequency systems have already transformed into light, which is another reason why we can no longer connect with them.

It is now up to each and every one of us to open our eyes, leave our old thinking behind, and start anew—begin thinking anew, begin acting anew, and allowing new possibilities into our lives that suddenly present themselves and have been waiting for us. It is up to us whether we finally leave what used to be the source of our security behind us.

I can say with certainty that these old and outdated forms of security have already ceased to exist at this time. Furthermore, I can say with certainty that there are new opportunities, new structures, and new frequencies waiting for us, as well as new people who we have not yet been able to meet.

The love in our hearts draws us to each other. We attract each other. And our love gives us the motivation to create something new, something based on loving and positive laws, something that will give security to our children and the generations to come, after our time.

Thank you all, dear readers and advocates of the radiant energies. Thank you for your energy work, for your support, and for your love.

My wish is that these texts may give you motivation for the next months of your glorious future. My wish for you is that, with the help of the "keys" in the following words, you will experience many moments of sudden insight and that your soul and your consciousness will decipher as much light information as possible, for your development and your existence.

I wish you much joy and happiness in the exploration of your earthly paths.

With love and gratitude!
Your Pavlina

Introduction from
the Pleiadians

Dear Messengers of Light! A new time, new healing, new techniques, new frequencies, and many new possibilities are waiting and opening up for all of you.

The new time you have all been waiting for has just begun. Perhaps some of you have been expecting the New Era to begin with something unexpected and revolutionary happening or appearing, something that no one could miss. Many of you expected the New Era would bring rapid changes from one day to the next. Many of you may have thought the changes would be so rapid and fast that it would be possible to exactly describe or perceive them.

The changes that occurred came through the back door, as it were; they approached you behind the scenes. The changes everyone has been waiting for opened times and spaces into new times and new spaces that will now lead you into a new, positive future.

We know how much strength, trust, and patience you have had to muster to prevent your personal light from going out or losing its intensity. We know how hard it is to hold the light at this time, when people around you or in your family have fallen into a state of mistrust, sorrow, grief, and fear. We know how much steadfastness and courage you have had to muster in order to remain an example and not lose your own strength. We know what a great task and what great responsibility you have taken on for this incarnation.

We know that the preparation for this incarnation in the dimensions of the heaven of human beings did not seem as dramatic to you as it feels now in this earthly reality. In the dimensions of the heaven of human beings, together with other human souls, you went over all the possible variations and all the possible situations that might await you during the time of your earthly incarnation. In the dimensions of light, you may not have realized that you would have to summon up so much personal power and show so much personal commitment in this incarnation.

We feel for you when we observe how much strength, patience, and endurance human beings have to call up. However, at the same time, we observe that human beings are being constantly reminded by the light beings not to forget their purest essence and to act according to their purest essence.

Many of you are currently experiencing one of your most significant incarnations on planet Earth. Many of you came to Earth to process your last karmic affairs. Many of you came to support your loved ones and the members of your family. Many of you have chosen to remember your personal light and your divine essence and being.

Many of you did not imagine that discovering your own divine essence on this earthly path would attract so many adventures. Little did you know that these adventures would often have an aftertaste of sadness, disappointment, defiance, anger, and resignation. You had no idea that recognizing the divine essence at this time would bring so many additional emotions—emotions that can only be felt when the human soul incarnates into a human body and lives through this incarnation on planet Earth.

Planet Earth is one of the planets where it is possible to process matters that led to the separation from the Divine Source in the history of earthly incarnations. A separation from the Divine Source entails a separation from yourself, from your own divine essence.

In this great, vast, infinite, divine happening, only two supreme laws apply: the law of unconditional love—to all others and to oneself—and the law of wholeness, of perfection. Through development, everything that has separated itself from this essence sets out on the path back to its own source—to its unconditional love and wholeness, its perfection.

Everything is made of love.

Love is the most powerful and highest element in all the events and all the development that lead toward perfection. The human community as a whole has lost its love for itself. It has lost its divine perfection and wholeness. It has separated itself from loving perfection and wholeness. Now it is on its way back—back to its essence, back to its love. This path is not easy. But never stop believing that, on this path, humanity will find its love and wholeness again.

Every individual walks their own path, and at the same time, through their existence, they contribute to the discovery of the divine essence of humanity as a whole.

Every individual walks their own path and illuminates the light of the whole with their light. Through this, they heal the karmic affairs of humankind as a whole.

Humanity, which has disconnected itself from the Divine Source and its love, will find its own path and its healing once more. It is necessary to trust for a while longer and not lose strength. It is necessary to know that the karmic affairs of humanity are being healed, and it is necessary to realize that each and every human being plays an indispensable role at this time.

Everything is striving toward love.

Everything is striving toward perfection. Humanity has embarked on this adventurous path, choosing to come to terms with and transform its dark and manipulated past once and for all.

Planet Earth, which is already in the fifth dimension of consciousness, is helping humanity with her light and with her love. She is helping humanity on its way to the light. She is helping humanity, through the power of nature and its beings, to find even more courage, both on the path to healing and in discovering its divine essence.

You have already come a long way. You have already traveled that part of the path that could be called the "path of courage." Maybe you remember this game from your childhood. Together with your friends, you set out on the path of courage, which was a great adventure for you. You played this game with full commitment, with full enthusiasm. You experienced it with all your senses, and yet you knew, in the depths of your soul, that this path of courage was only a game, and you knew that this adventure game would eventually end.

You all knew this adventure would only bring you pleasure on condition that, at the end of this path, your destination was waiting for you and you could breathe a common sigh of relief and enjoy the impressions you had collected along the adventurous path. You knew you would be able to remember your experiences with ease and joy. You knew the path of courage was only a game.

Your path on this planet will also bring you to a destination, and you will know for certain that although this path has been demanding, it has been worth the effort. This is certain.

Once you arrive at your destination, you will know that the experiences you have had have connected you even more deeply with the divine essence, its light, love, and perfection.

You will know that each experience has brought you a luminous stone to place in the mosaic of the light world of your soul. You will know that each and every experience has connected your mind more and more with the synapses of the galactic event and to its positive matrix. You will know that your body has illuminated its substance, because your soul and mind have absorbed a huge amount of light-filled impulses during their healing process.

You will know that your strength has paid off and your heavenly plan for your incarnation on this planet has been fulfilled. Your soul will be content because it did not disappoint other human souls with whom it had planned the course of this incarnation.

Now we are off on an adventure with you once more. We will accompany you, and we will strengthen you with light and energy on the earthly path of your incarnation. We look forward to the light-filled connection that will bring further love into our hearts. We are indescribably grateful that, on your way to the light, you are also supporting other civilizations in this galaxy that are in a similar situation and phase as the human community.

Believe that your path will be successful. Believe that when you look back, you will see the results and the progress of your work. Every positive deed, every positive thought, and every positive emotion has brought you a little further forward.

Follow the light. Follow the love. Follow your perfection and your wholeness. Follow the wholeness and the reunion with the Divine Source.

We are with you. We support you. We love you.

Your Pleiadian Community

PART ONE

Messages in the
Field of Healing

1

The Time–Space of Cosmic Freedom,
the Effects of the Manipulation of
Humankind, and a Liberating Solution

At this time, great energetic changes are pending that will contribute to the overall ascent into the light-filled dimensions of the consciousness-based era.

These changes will shift the human mind and soul into the original realms, where they were last when they had the purest connection to Divine Intelligence, during the course of their incarnations in a human body on Earth.

It is difficult to compare the overall forward progress in past years with the present time. In past years, progress toward the light on the energy level took place slowly and ponderously. Due to the currently increased presence of cosmic light on this planet, processes are moving quickly, and the human mind is able to connect to the light frequency of this galaxy with its own vibration.

Correspondingly, the human soul has been given the opportunity, by virtue of its purest essence and light, to connect with other human beings of pure essence, thereby amplifying the light of this planet and the human community.

Even though the dark forces are still trying to preserve the nets they have spread over the whole planet, the freedom of the human mind and soul is difficult to repress. Despite the presence of the dark beings' nets and traps, the human mind and soul can choose the spaces and times they wish to move in. They do not have to move in the spaces of time in which the nets and traps of the dark powers and beings are located.

The human mind and the human soul cannot be captured or bound. Through the power of their own will and freedom, they can move in the spaces and times they consider to be appropriate. They can move in the spaces and times in which the minds and spirits of most human beings move *in the spaces and times of cosmic freedom.* These spaces and times of cosmic freedom are an essential element with regard to what is happening in the cosmos. In these spaces and times, human beings with a free will meet in thought and feeling. They will meet and experience their personal freedom here until the human community has been fully liberated.

Do not forget that each one of you has this possibility, and that each one of you is connected to the element and frequency of cosmic freedom.

The dark beings and dark powers that have controlled human beings to their advantage are leaving this planet quickly. Their existence on this planet is already as good as over. For a long time, with the help of the mass media, they managed to control a large number of human beings and, basically, almost all of what was happening on this planet.

The number of dark beings on this planet has already greatly decreased. From our standpoint, we can see that only about 5–10 percent of the beings on this planet at the moment are dark-thinking beings of extraterrestrial origin, but because they control a large section of the mass media, it looks as if their presence and numbers are invincible and unstoppable.

The negative-thinking extraterrestrial beings that have directed political, pharmaceutical, economic, and banking circles know that the light on planet Earth and the growth of consciousness of human beings will more or less force them to leave this planet or reprogram themselves to the positive.

The human community is progressing, step by step, into new levels of consciousness. The number of awakened human souls necessary for this progress to take place was already reached by the end of 2020. Now, it is only a matter of the speed with which headway is made along the path to the light.

The dark beings and dark powers that negatively control human beings know that the light-filled consciousness evolution is detrimental to them. They are therefore still developing plans to enable them, with the quickest possible speed, to hold the population trapped within a form of manipulation and maintain emotions of fear and panic.

Human beings who do not know how to move with their mind and soul into the spaces of their personal freedom have already succumbed to the pressure of the mass media. The manipulation of the dark forces was so strong that their minds and souls lost their agility and flexibility and became subordinate to the heaviness and manipulation of the dark forces.

Many human beings have succumbed to their lies and meanness as a result. The good nature of human beings, as well as their social behavior and solidarity with others, has been exploited.

Until now, the political, pharmaceutical, economic, and banking concerns have, hand in hand, been manipulating humanity for such a long time now. Many human beings have succumbed, in particular, to pharmaceutical pressure or have not seen through this trap. They have not recognized the concomitant effects of manipulation. Out of solidarity or consideration for others, they have allowed their bodies to be influenced by chemical and genetic substances that did not originate on this planet. These manipulative substances were created in the laboratories of extraterrestrial, negative civilizations beyond this planet.

The effects are sensed not only by the human body but also by the human soul. Not feeling comfortable in a manipulated body, the human soul gradually fragments itself. In its normal state, the soul is in 100 percent contact and communication with the body.

Soul, mind, and body are one. After the intervention of this chemical and genetic information, the soul of the human being ceases to be in absolute contact and communication with the body. *Their fragments are located in dimensions created by the dark beings for this purpose.*

The human community, which is in the process of settling its karmic affairs, is experiencing this situation directly, literally firsthand. In the process, however, the global situation is bringing back the memory of personal intuition, power, and natural essence to a large number of human beings.

Thanks to this situation, many people are remembering who they truly are. They are remembering that no one has the right to make decisions about their health, their state of being, their actions, and their existence.

We are convinced that this situation will awaken many human beings, and these awakened human beings will then begin to act and take responsibility for their bodies, minds, and souls.

The manipulations that have taken place, and are still taking place, are enormous. They have been happening on this planet for thousands of years, and we have told you many times that Divine Intelligence has allowed the Cosmic Council and peace-loving extraterrestrial civilizations to help in certain areas of the human community for this reason.

Behind the scenes, countless steps are being taken, preparations are being made for the launch of new technologies that will help the human community "stand on its own two feet" again. Technologies are being prepared to help regenerate and heal the substance of human beings and their DNA. Many human beings who have come to Earth with the purpose of helping to build a new community are already waiting in the wings.

The human community is being helped on the energetic level—not only have incredible numbers of light beings descended to the planet but the human community is also receiving energetic support from peace-loving extraterrestrial civilizations.

Divine Intelligence has prepared an even greater amount of help for the human civilization than even we imagined. Since June 2020, we have seen grace, the healing of God, coming to human beings. We see a beautiful, light-blue light that comes specifically to those human beings who have succumbed to manipulation and who, out of a sense of solidarity with others, have allowed their bodies to be influenced by foreign substances. This grace comes to people of pure heart and to people who carry human goodness and love for others within them.

The soul fragments lost by these human beings will be returned at the appropriate time to those who have woken up. In the near future, groups of people will come together who will focus on collective healing, and these same healers will be wonderful helpers when it comes to the overall healing of the human community.

At this time, many human beings have chosen to take a longer path in their incarnation. However, some have chosen a shorter path in their incarnation, because the time they have spent on this planet has been sufficient for them to work through the issues they set out to address.

They knew this time would be favorable, because during this time an increased number of cosmic healing frequencies and light would be coming to the planet.

Many of these people only came to this planet in the first place to finish and complete "the game" they had started playing in their past incarnations.

Do not forget that this global situation is part of the plan for the healing and restoration of karmic human affairs. Every person has a certain role to play and every person influences others. Every decision, even the decision to leave this planet, is part of the overall plan and is beneficial for the overall healing of the human community as a whole.

Every human being who has chosen this present incarnation on this planet has chosen not only their own healing and enlightenment but, through their presence here, also the healing and enlightenment of the whole.

Every decision and every situation lived through in this time and space on planet Earth contributes to the increased illumination of the human community as a whole. The light of the soul of each person illuminates the spaces of their reality and connects with the light of the realities of other human beings.

Healing and processing the karmic situation of humanity as a whole would not have been at all possible in earlier times. The cosmic conditions, the constellation of planet Earth, and the influx of cosmic light to planet Earth and to the other inhabited planets of this galaxy are what have made this process possible. During this time, thousands of inhabited planets in this galaxy are emerging from their dark past reality. The Cosmic Council and the extraterrestrial civilizations of goodwill are also accompanying these civilizations from a distance, and equally energetically, because all of the planets and their populations will ascend into higher dimensions of consciousness at about the same time as the human civilization.

You all influence each other.

Believe that every positive thought, emotion, and deed influences the ascent of other civilizations that are in the same or similar evolution. All of the planets belong to the matrix of this galaxy, and all of the galaxies and their systems belong to the matrix of the Divine Source.

All is returning to the original order.

All is returning to divine order.

Even the dark beings, which at the moment are influencing human civilization negatively, are going through a development that will lead them back to their divine origin. The dark beings are also experiencing difficult times in their development, because they intuitively sense that a return to the divine system entails restorative measures that will not always be pleasant.

In previous publications, we explained that the dark negative beings also originated in the Divine Source. However, their development was accompanied by different energetic influences to those accompanying the positive beings. We informed you that their development was due to a curvature of the planes, which occurred as a result of a shift in the matrix systems.

However, these beings also originated in the divine light and in the divine world. And their development will likewise end in the system of the divine order. But they will first have to go through their process of development and bear the consequences of their behavior. The consequences for them will most likely consist in processing dark frequencies of all kinds that they have attracted to themselves through their negative deeds.

In the near future, the human community will experience situations that will bring all people of goodwill together, to an even greater extent. Seen from this perspective, the dark beings play a karmic role, enabling human beings to better remember and to begin communicating with each other, using the power of purest intention from a pure heart. The dark beings have taken on this role, which will ultimately help the human community to free itself from negative influences, precisely at this time.

We therefore advise you, from the bottom of our hearts: Observe and perceive this situation from the perspective of your higher consciousness. By looking at the entire planetary situation from a higher perspective, you will more easily be able to see that everything is going according to plan and that every being on this planet—whether positive or negative—is playing its rightful role. Positive beings receive and distribute cosmic light on Earth, and negative beings, through their behavior, bring back to human beings the memory of their purest essence.

The process of karmic restoration and healing of the human community is already in full swing. Try to perceive this process—as we never tire of saying—from a higher perspective of your higher consciousness. This will spare you disappointments, as well as expectations that cannot be fulfilled, with regard to the particular actions and deeds of diverse human beings.

Let this process run. Let it run, and focus on the purest essence in your soul. Focus on your thoughts, which can help you assess a wide variety of situations from a positive point of view. Focus on your body, and give it rest, a healthy light diet, and time to be in nature. Focus on the vision of your personal positive future. Bless those human beings who are harming you at the moment. Through the power of your blessing, ascribe to them at least part of the healing process through your words and intention.

In the future, collective meditations and collective healings will be needed to heal your human colleagues who have had their bodies genetically manipulated because of their good nature. Thanks to your collective work, it will be possible to heal them and retrieve their soul fragments.

These collective meditations will be needed throughout the whole planet. It will be necessary to increase the overall light vibration of humanity as a whole to enable it to shed the burdens it carries within. We too freed ourselves in this way, in earlier phases of the dark past. We carried out global meditations and healings that allowed us to ascend from those burdensome low-vibrational levels. In this way, we healed the systems of our planetary inhabitants who had succumbed to the manipulations of the dark forces in earlier times.

We are aware that many human beings have decided to leave their corporeal sheath. But these beings will be helped by your collective light, and they will be given the opportunity to heal their soul systems. This will enable them to descend to this planet in their next incarnation free of any major burdens.

Peace be with you.
Peace be with us.

2

The Grace of God Taking Place in the Heaven of Human Beings and the Children of the Future

The grace of God, already mentioned, will positively affect and influence countless areas relating to humanity. Because human individuals are receiving divine healing, other systems of human existence will be healed.

At this time, when it seems to some human beings that there is no escape from their current situation, the healing of the Divine Source, which is the highest form of healing, is being given.

The first rays of this supreme healing have already reached your planet. They are the first drops of light coming directly from the Divine Source. Until now, the human being had to consciously connect to the Divine Source for healing contact to be established. Since June 2021, you have been receiving the grace of God, receiving the healing of God without actively invoking it.

This is the very greatest gift that the human community can receive. The first drops of the light of divine healing have already reached you, and more and more will be arriving in the coming time. This fact will affect the whole community.

Because the light of God's healing grace has begun to descend upon the planet, another giant step has been taken toward the unstoppable victory over the dark karmic burdens of humanity, a step toward the healing of the human soul, the human mind, and the human substance.

In this way, God's grace is bringing you very positive conditions, enabling further successful processes in the overall liberation of the community, as well as in the construction of new forms of community that will serve all beings positively.

The younger generation of your children will help you greatly in the process of building new structures. It will close the gates to humanity's dark past, once and for all. This new generation of children, who are still preparing for their incarnation, will bring increased frequencies of cosmic love and other positive frequencies from the Divine Source, because their connection to the Divine Source and its positive laws will be stable and unimaginably loving.

The grace of God that is now coming to human beings is also shining through other systems of human civilization. It is not only coming to those human beings who are incarnated in their present body; it is also coming to those human souls who are in the heaven of human beings at this moment.

Divine healing is penetrating their souls and cleansing their matrix, in which dark emotions from memories of experiences of the manipulated past are stored. Thanks to the divine healing light, many human souls in the heaven of human beings are being helped at this time to release, once and for all, the traumas and blockages that prevent human souls from ascending to the light-filled levels of the heavenly world.

Human souls who suffered greatly from the manipulations of the dark forces during their lifetime on Earth are being healed and, in the divine light, their burdens are finally being transformed. At the same time, energetic imprints of their experiences in the dark past are being transformed, allowing them to detach themselves from the energy of their burdening earthly incarnations and not be bound by energetic ties between them and Earth, and the people who are still on Earth.

Perhaps members of your family have also suffered during their lifetime on Earth from the manipulations of the political and social systems introduced by dark-thinking beings. Perhaps it is important for you to know that your family members and ancestors are currently receiving increased divine healing and will finally be able to release their memories and the blockages that burden them.

This privilege was not possible in earlier times. In earlier times, processing a wide variety of karmic matters meant an enormous number of earthly incarnations. The karmic issues created by the manipulation of the dark forces are being subjected to divine correction, as well as to God's grace in the heaven of human beings, at this very time.

We observe that the heaven of human beings and the human souls residing there are becoming enveloped in a beautiful light-blue, luminous, soft blanket that harmonizes the manipulative elements of the human past.

We wish you could experience the feelings of infinite gratitude and relief of these human souls that are now being given the highest form of healing. What great love and what great light there is in the souls of those human beings who can expand the light of their souls and connect in a light-filled and loving manner with other human souls nearby.

They are being given the opportunity to connect lovingly and full of light to light beings with which they had no connection, in terms of vibration, in past times, because the light and love of their soul was not sufficient. Human souls in the heaven of human beings are experiencing a heightened sense of happiness, because they are aware that their lives will be free of the burdens from those manipulative times when they next descend to Earth.

They will be able to process karmic issues concerning personal development and not related to manipulation during their next stay on Earth. But know that almost all these karmic issues were of manipulated origin, which means the remaining karmic issues are infinitesimal, and therefore easy to deal with.

And do not forget that those human souls that will be incarnating on planet Earth in the near future will increasingly carry the light of the Divine Source within them, and therefore carry increased consciousness and increased light in their soul.

It is possible that close family members preparing to incarnate soon are also among the New Children of the New Era, who are bringing to this planet the increased divine light and new knowledge that will help not only your earthly family but also the entire human community.

The children of the New Era are connected with each other in frequency and light. They know of each other. They know of the presence of the others, and they know of the possibilities that await them in the future.

Through the gifts of God's grace and divine healing, the human community is being helped to step out of the manipulated past; it is being helped to ascend to new light-filled dimensions of consciousness.

At this time, in this time–space, you have not yet had any clear idea of what life will be like and how things will be in your future. We can say with certainty that the divine guardian energy and its intelligence are watching over the human community.

Everyone who is ready to accept this helping guardian energy and "helping hand" will be given the opportunity to ascend to new dimensions of consciousness, of which they would never have even dared to dream of until now.

Sooner or later, the third dimension of consciousness on this planet will be transformed. From about the year 2030, it will no longer be possible for lower forms of consciousness and lower-vibrational beings to incarnate on this planet or to function or exist here. On Earth, a radiant and loving future awaits those who have chosen a light-filled and loving way of life.

Peace be with you.
Peace be with us.

3

The Illusion of Human Destinies and a New Number Sequence for Liberation from the Manipulation of the Past

The manipulations of the dark beings and powers have affected the whole human community. However, please do not forget—not ever—that the light-filled frequencies and rays have greater power and resilience than the dark elements. Everything strives toward the light and into the light. That is why this development toward the light on Earth is inexorable.

In their souls, many human beings still suffer today from the manipulations that took place, and it has not been possible for them to understand the origin of their sufferings. Many human beings have not yet realized that their suffering is not necessarily always caused by experiences in earthly incarnations.

That is understandable because the human mind, in the reality of its earthly incarnation, considers this reality to be indisputable. The human mind can connect with the elements of the past, but it is unable to discern whether the experiences and visions that flow to it are real or artificially created.

With these sentences, we would like to share with you another part of the truth that will come to the surface sooner or later. We will reveal the truth step by step, to the extent that human beings can grasp it. We will reveal the truth step by step to make it possible for the human mind, the human soul, and ultimately, the human body to process the truth and the healing frequency of the truth.

We are aware that many human beings will have problems grasping and processing the following information. However, we are also aware that the truth will open the gates to the healing of the human community and the healing of each individual. We are aware that we can only convey the truth in small portions, because the realization of the great truth will bring with it an awakening of human perception in every sense. The truth can be painful but also healing at the same time. This depends on the extent to which the human being has already discovered and processed their own personal truth. To the extent they have done so, the more open they will be to understanding the truth concerning the global situation of humanity and its history.

In recent years, the history of humankind and its line of development has often been bent, interrupted, multiplied, steered, and moved in a direction that was favorable to the dark powers.

The history of humankind is different from what has been handed down to you in history books or textbooks. Not all the events told of and passed down from generation to generation took place. Not all the events the human community takes at face value, in their present time, took place in the way described.

The human community has been manipulated, its consciousness lowered, and its brain capacity diminished. The health and longevity of human beings have been reduced.

The development of the human community took place under different circumstances and conditions to what you have always believed. The Middle Ages stretched farther through the timeline and spatial axis of humanity than is stated in history books. The Middle Ages lasted longer than the other epochs of human evolution.

It was stretched temporally and its duration extended.

The period of the Middle Ages, with its horrors, has been deeply engraved on the memory of humankind. At the same time, situations were encoded in the memory of human beings, which constantly cause them to feel guilt. You all know that human beings are not able to find self-love within themselves if they are burdened with guilt for their actions. And low self-love prevents human beings from connecting with divine love, the highest love there is.

The lives, lifelines, and temporal axes of every human being who has gone through incarnations here on Earth have been manipulated. Not only the period of the Middle Ages but also the repeatedly interrupted axis of the human community gave the dark beings the opportunity and power to encode memories and visions in the human mind at the moment of the interruption of the time axis, blocking human beings in their development and in their realization of the "great truth," which is still being hidden from the human community.

People have had memories encoded in their minds that they believe they actually lived through karmically.

Almost every person—especially those who wish to develop their consciousness—processes karmic issues in order to detach themselves from the dark past they have experienced. For many people, processing these karmic issues is a lengthy business, and they often do not succeed in removing these karmic issues from their system. This means that many human beings are striving to free themselves once and for all.

You may have begun to realize that a great many karmic memories you think you actually experienced may not have happened at all, even though they seem real to you.

Healers who "read" your karmic memories may not be able to tell if the images of your past are real or not. This is very understandable because the images of your past that have been artificially encoded in your systems show up as situations actually experienced. In this way, the dark-thinking beings have manipulated not only your personal past but the entire human past and your perception of it. As a result, many of you perceive and evaluate your own karmic past as negative.

Many of you believe this illusion because the images of this illusion present themselves as being true and real. Many of you believe you were a bad person in the past and often suffer from feelings of guilt.

Many of you, because of these manipulative, artificially encoded thoughts, visions, and perceptions, carry negative programs that are not yours at all. Many of your points of view and programs were given to you artificially, so that even today, you still believe that the events of your past happened the way you think they did.

This illusion, about which we have often written, permeates all the realities of humankind. This illusion, which existed and partly still exists in the thoughts of human beings, will be transformed over the coming years.

The artificially created morphogenetic fields and dimensions of illusion, to which the dark forces tethered the human mind and system, no longer exist. Archangel Metatron was allowed by Divine Intelligence to transform the corresponding fields and dimensions. The illusion still exists in your mind and personal systems, but you are no longer tethered to these fields and dimensions or connected to them.

Now the important thing—and we have told you this many times before—is to illuminate your personal reality and transform negativities. When you illuminate your reality, you free yourself from these manipulative burdens because the dimensions and fields of these artificially created memories and illusions no longer exist.

Perhaps it is easier for you to understand if I say that you can close the door to your past (and therefore, the artificially created past) behind you, once and for all. You can now focus on your present and your positive future!

During this time you will receive increased support from the light beings. You will receive healing, light-filled power, and information that will make it easier for you to understand that it is possible for you to find your purest human essence again and that this is real.

You will receive information that will help you understand that all human beings are pure beings who carry the divine light within them. Every human being carries the divine light within. Maybe some have simply forgotten their light. Maybe some have forgotten their light only partially or for a time. But the divine light, which every human being carries within, cannot be ignored—and this light shows itself to human beings in every moment.

The information coming to you enables you to understand that each one of you is the purest divine essence. It enables you to understand that humanity's past was manipulated and you were given feelings of guilt that do not let you live freely. This guilt has affected your past incarnations, and it has also affected your present life.

It is time to rid yourself, once and for all, of the illusions that do not belong to you— the illusions that have been artificially fed to you and clouded the systems of your reality and the systems of your personal perception; the illusions that have interfered with your systems and burdened the systems of your families and your human collective.

Maybe the illusion, whose artificially created morphogenetic fields and dimensions have long since ceased to exist, is still flashing through your mind. It is a variable parameter that has been abused by the dark forces. This illusion causes you to live in low-vibrational spaces, even though these spaces have not been where you rightfully belong for a long time.

This illusion makes you live a life that does not belong in the fifth dimension of consciousness.

The dark beings have used the formative qualities of the frequency of this illusion to change your lives and your perception, the perception of others, and the perception of yourselves.

This illusion has given you images, mirages, and programs that do not belong to you in any way.

This is how they did it. If the time axis is interrupted, a dimensional space resembling a huge bubble is created. This bubble has properties that enable it to encode an enormous amount of information within itself—information transmitted to it by sophisticated technological devices. This bubble, programmed with new information, has the ability to connect to every human being on the planet through its intelligence. By this means, the information contained in it is projected onto every human being, with the result that the new, artificially created reality appears real to everyone.

Holographic programs are used, which are fed directly into a human being's personal system. The programs in the minds of human beings are transferred via energetic imprints. It is possible to transmit thoughts in the same way, because thoughts are vibrating programs and are variable. It is enough to "tune" the person in question to a certain vibration—for example, fear, hatred, guilt, or remorse—for that person to then attract these thought programs more and more. (We have told you repeatedly that low-vibrational thoughts do not come from your mind; every human being is a pure divine being.)

Basically, the interruption of the time axis, at which time memories and visions are encoded in the human mind, only takes a split second; you would not even be necessarily aware of it. The dark beings perform these actions specifically during times when the human community is caught up in certain global events and the inhabitants of Earth are emotionally shaken. During such times, people subliminally connect in terms of consciousness through the collective field.

One such timeline interruption in your recent past occurred, for example, on September 11, 2001. The panic and fear were exploited, and no one realized that programs were encoded in the timeline that negatively affected the following years for humanity on this planet.

An interruption of the timeline has been implemented several times during your history without any of you noticing. This is because the time it takes is just a split second in the course of your time.

The technologies used for this are currently still beyond human comprehension. What has been achieved by means of these technologies is that the human community has not developed in terms of consciousness as it would naturally have done. At this time, however, you are receiving so much cosmic light that it is, and will be, no longer possible to work negatively on this planet, because this cosmic light neutralizes everything that is negative.

That is a cosmic law.

Transmission of a New Number Sequence

To support you, we would now like to transmit another number sequence that will help you to transform any artificially created visions and programs that are not your own.

This number sequence holds great power. It is connected to information fields that help you neutralize artificially created visions and programs of illusion in your systems, and dissolve dark, low-vibrational particles of these programs into light. The intensity of the transformation adapts automatically, because this numerical code carries its own intelligence (as do the other number sequences we have shared with you, by the way). The artificially created visions and programs that have been unnaturally encoded in your systems will be transformed in divine light.

Thanks to the new number sequence, you will be able to free yourself, step by step, from the past that has burdened you and is not yours at all.

The number sequence is:

57819

The above sequence of digits is very important for you at this time. It will help you rid yourselves of negative memories and programs you perceive to be real. It is almost unbelievable how much these non-real memories have influenced humankind and the whole human community. In the present situation, we have been able to see with our own eyes what manipulation can do to a pure human being.

This number sequence is also capable of reprogramming your personal negative programs. This is possible because the artificially created programs are naturally interwoven with your own personal programs.

To do this, however, we would now like to give you some necessary guidance as follows:

It is necessary to reprogram your whole system of perception; specifically, your perception of your soul, mind, body, and energy body, or aura. In reprogramming your energy body, or aura, it is enough to see your aura as a whole; it is not necessary to go into various parts and layers of your energy bodies. This number sequence is programmed to purify your aura as a whole.

As you reprogram your negative memories, visions, and programs, they may initially worsen. This is often referred to as a healing crisis. It addition, as you let go of these negativities, as these emotions and thoughts depart, you may feel tearful, unable to sleep, disappointment, anger, or similar reactions. It is also possible, and even likely, that you may experience certain reactions or sensations of pressure in various places throughout the body.

By working with the above number sequence, your cellular memory will purify itself. Your cells will release negativities that have burdened them. They will be able to increase their light vibration and once again absorb the pure energy of Earth and the cosmos. Harmful programs have accompanied you from incarnation to incarnation and occupied your cellular memory. It is time to remove these faulty programs and negativities from your cells and from your whole system.

At this time, reprogramming to tune in to light energy and light information will be easier for you because you are surrounded by the purest cosmic light. This will help you to keep your system radiant and pure.

Only program your system when you are consciously ready for it. If you feel that a part of you still wants to remain in its present state, do not use this number sequence until you feel quite clearly that you have voluntarily chosen to embrace absolute personal freedom.

Those of you who have already been working on personal growth will be able to apply this number sequence straightaway, because you will have already been focusing on the question of personal freedom and a positive future and what that will look like when you reach a phase of heightened consciousness development. You have moved forward, step by step, and now have a clear idea of the direction in which you are moving. You have oriented yourselves toward the positive, and step by step, reprogrammed your systems to receive radiant, positive energy.

Those of you working with our Pleiadian techniques for the first time must consider whether you are ready for the reality of this concrete positive reprogramming. If the process we offer here is too fast for you, make sure you first understand the task of your chakras and begin to program them positively (for example, with the affirmations and exercises for the chakras from my previous book, *Light Messages from the Pleiades*).

You can also program your drinking water with this new number sequence and then observe how your system reacts when you drink it. If the positive reaction is too strong for you, stop drinking the programmed water or drink it intuitively, as needed and according to the intensity of your reaction.

After programming your system, you may feel or sense a gap, or empty space, that wants to be filled with positive elements. For this, you can do the Fountain of Light exercise after freeing your system from all negativities.

Freeing Your System from Harmful Programs

For those of you who have decided to reprogram your system *now and in this space,* and who have decided to rid yourselves of artificially encoded negativities, visions, and programs, we offer the following process:

1. Reprogramming and Releasing Negativities from the System of Your Soul

Take a sheet of green paper and, at the top, write the number sequence **57819** in gold, a color that can transform negative programs in your system. The shade of green of the paper is not important. Whatever the shade, it will carry the vibration of healing for your soul.

Your eyes, with which you perceive this green, are the gateways to your soul and, through this green, your soul is enabled to reprogram and heal itself. Your soul is now gradually releasing faulty programs, step by step.

Now write the following affirmation under the number sequence in gold:

> "I (your first name) contact my soul in the here and now.
>
> My intention is pure and clear.
>
> My soul, please release all negativities and programs that burden you in all times and all spaces of my reality.
>
> I (your first name) allow you to do this. I am absolutely determined to purify, heal, and connect to cosmic freedom.
>
> Bless you. I love you.
>
> Thank you, thank you, thank you."

Now look at the golden number sequence **57819** on the green sheet in front of you for three minutes and then consciously repeat the affirmation below it at least three times in a row.

2. Reprogramming and Releasing Negativities from the System of Your Mind

In order to reprogram your mind to focus on the positive, use a sheet of red paper and, at the top, write the number sequence **57819** in gold.

The shade of red is not important. Whatever the shade, the vibration of the red color neutralizes faulty programs in your brain region. Your eyes, with which you perceive the red color, connects you with your soul, and your soul passes the information to your mind.

Now write the following affirmation under this number sequence in gold:

"I (your first name) contact my mind in the here and now.

My intention is pure and clear.

My mind, please release all negativities and programs that burden you in all times and all spaces of my reality.

I (your first name) allow you to do this. I am absolutely determined to purify, heal, and connect to cosmic freedom.

Bless you. I love you.

Thank you, thank you, thank you."

Now look at the golden number sequence **57819** on the red sheet in front of you for three minutes and then consciously repeat the above affirmation at least three times in a row.

3. Reprogramming and Releasing Negativities from the System of Your Body

In order to positively reprogram your body, at the top of a white sheet of paper write the number sequence **57819** in gold. The vibration of the white color helps your body release encoded negativities. Your eyes, with which you perceive the white, connects you with the intelligence of your body.

Now write the following affirmation under the number sequence in gold:

"I (your first name) contact the intelligence of my body in the here and now.

My intention is pure and clear.

My body, please release all negativities and programs that are burdening you in all times and all spaces of my reality.

I (your first name) allow you to do this. I am absolutely determined to purify, heal, and connect to cosmic freedom.

Bless you. I love you.

Thank you, thank you, thank you."

Now look at the number sequence **57819** in gold on the white sheet in front of you for three minutes and then consciously repeat the affirmation at least three times in a row.

4. Reprogramming and Releasing Negativities from the System of Your Energy Body

For this positive reprogramming, write the number sequence **57819** in purple at the top of a light-blue sheet of paper. The frequencies of the purple color bring clearing purification to your energy body, and the light-blue color that your eyes behold brings it divine healing.

Now, also in purple, write the following affirmation under the number sequence:

> "I (your first name) contact the intelligence of my energy body in the here and now.
>
> My intention is pure and clear.
>
> My energy body, please release all negativities and programs that are burdening you in all times and all spaces of my reality.
>
> I (your first name) allow you to do this. I am absolutely determined to purify, heal, and connect to cosmic freedom.
>
> Bless you. I love you.
>
> Thank you, thank you, thank you."

Now look at the purple number sequence **57819** on the light-blue background in front of you for three minutes and then consciously repeat the affirmation at least three times in a row.

5. The Light Fountain Exercise

After working with the number sequence and affirmations for all your systems, do the following exercise. It is called the Light Fountain. With its help, you can optimize the whole process. Your whole system can settle down and, filled with light, reprogram, regenerate, and heal. The places in your system that have released negativities can now be filled with luminous information.

To do this exercise, proceed as follows:

Imagine that golden light is reaching your crown chakra from the cosmos. This golden light enters your crown chakra and flows down into your heart.

Now imagine that through the soles of your feet the purest light and energy of Earth is entering and also flowing to your heart.

Imagine this energy in golden color as well.

The light energy of the cosmos and Earth meet in your heart. Their current is so strong that you can watch a fountain of light emerge from your heart.

The rays of this light flow in all directions and into all the spaces of your body and aura.

They flow into all the spaces of your existence.

You can let the light of these rays expand in any direction.

Now visualize this glorious light for as long as your intuition tells you to.

6. Programming Water

You can also program water with this number sequence. To do this, use a white piece of paper and write **57819** at the top in gold. By drawing the sign of infinity on all four sides, you make sure that this number sequence can still carry on working in your system afterwards. Transmit this information to the water for at least three minutes, and drink it in sips as needed.

∞

8 57819 8

∞

You can carry on doing this reprogramming with the help of the number sequence, affirmations, and drinking the programmed water until you feel free from negativities and negative programs. This depends on the strength of the manipulation in your system.

We thank you for your valuable work and for the liberation of your system.

Peace be with you.
Peace be with us.

4

New Crop Circle and Information on Free Energy

Message from the Pleiadian Civilization about This Phenomenon!

In August 2021, a new crop circle was created in Buchendorf, above Gauting, south of Munich, Germany. As with the crop circle in Fischen, which we told you about in *Light Messages from the Pleiades*, it is simple and at the same time enormously healing. Once again, the energy flow has a radius of several kilometers, and it also reaches several kilometers into Earth's interior.

In this manifestation, there are circles, which show yet again how important the symbolism of the circle is, because everything is made of circles. Through looking at the circles, the systems of your mind, soul, body, and energy body heal. The circles in this crop circle represent the endlessness and at the same time the simplicity of the universe. Everything is ordered, everything is repeated, and everything has its cosmic order. Everything is simple and at the same time powerful and magical.

This crop circle carries the energy and message from our Pleiadian civilization, which is as follows:

We are with you. We love you. Soon, a time will dawn when we will be allowed to come to you physically. Soon, a time will dawn when we will meet in the symbolism of the circle. The circle connects us. Its endlessness connects us. The circle encompasses all that happens, all love, and all light information. Consider the shape of the circle. Observe its symbolism. It connects us. It puts us in touch with each other. Circle, circles. The energy of the circle.

As long as there are still cracks in your human reality and consciousness created by the negative programming that took place in you during interruptions in the timeline, we are not allowed to enter your earthly reality. Once the energy of human consciousness and the human community begins to flow in a circular fashion, we will be allowed by the Cosmic Council to enter your reality, on planet Earth. Rid yourselves of all those energies that do not feel "round" and that block you. You are on a good path. We are with you.

Use the symbolism of the manifestation in the cornfield for your healing. Everything is contained in these circles, your cardinal points as well, absolutely everything—your essence, your being, your existence. And not only your existence but also the existence of divine love and its intelligence and the essence of everything that happens.

The Pleiadians Talking about Free Energy

On this occasion we would like to convey to you some information concerning free energy, which has been withheld from you for so long.

Our technical achievements use the magic and the power of circularly spinning free energy. At the same time, we use magnetic conductors that open times and spaces that we want to connect with or that offer us the opportunity to fulfill our needs. Everything works together with the frequency and the magnitude of love and gratitude and is bound up with it.

Our pure hearts also open these energetic spaces, and we can enter them, work in them, and exist in them.

The most important condition determining our life and the use of cosmic spaces is our pure heart, which enables us to use free energy. The cosmic plasma contained in free energy offers us all the possibilities we need. But it is important to understand that plasma—cosmic plasma—is a divine magnitude and has its own intelligence. We are not allowed to use plasma for purposes that do not serve all of us as a whole, as a collective.

In order to be allowed to use the cosmic plasma contained in free energy, it is important to feel and indicate that this substance will only be used for the purest purposes—purposes that serve us all.

Cosmic plasma has the ability to expand infinitely, but it is also capable of gathering its volume into a miniature space. It is able to communicate with the consciousness of any being that comes into contact with it. It is capable of tracing the shape of any object as well as any being absolutely realistically.

Your human "doubles," which are absolutely convincing imprints of the original form, and which are used for the most diverse purposes, in most cases consist of this plasma; however, using cosmic plasma for purposes that do not correspond to the divine order— playing with it, in that sense—is not in accordance with the higher cosmic laws of the consciousness of Divine Intelligence.

The use of cosmic plasma for purposes that do not serve the purest intention is thwarted sooner or later, because the plasma then returns to its original light-filled energy. Cosmic plasma is more intelligent than any beings that use it for their negative purposes. Modulated cosmic plasma is free energy brought into form and always has the tendency to return to its original form. It can also decide to expand again to its original size and thereby destroy its creator through its infinite power.

Not everyone is allowed to work with plasma. Anyone who risks using plasma negatively for personal gain is really playing with fire.

The human community is in a process of evolution that is moving toward the use of free energy. Technologies based on the operating principle of free energy have already been made ready for the human community. These are technologies that will help humanity to return to their original health and to their original divine frequency. But for this, it is necessary to purify your heart and raise your consciousness. Human beings will then be able to connect with the original divine imprint they left behind in the Divine Source.

Technologies based on the principle of free energy for the healing of humankind function very simply. A particular magnetic frequency initiates a rotating motion of the plasma particles. Owing to its intelligence, the plasma contained in free energy can instantly connect with the person to be healed and simultaneously connect that person to their divine imprint.

In every particle of light there is information about the divine origin of every human being, because every particle of light comes from the Divine Source. Through this information, free energy connects the person to be healed with Divine Intelligence, and in so doing, creates that person's absolute, divine, energetic imprint, which in turn connects with their reality.

In this way, it is possible to heal a person's body and purify their soul and mind from negativities. Someone who has activated the sacred chamber in their heart is able to heal and regenerate faster than someone who is still seeking elevated consciousness. But such people can also be helped, especially with regard to their health. By regaining their physical health, their soul and mind are able to connect better and more quickly to the dimensions of higher consciousness.

Even without the technologies that are still waiting for the human community, human beings that have activated the sacred chamber in their hearts have the potential to regenerate, heal, and connect to their source more quickly. This sacred chamber connects them with the Divine Source. The sacred chamber of their heart—this miniature chamber within their heart—is filled with free energy, which connects them with the Divine Source and their potentials.

Through the sacred chamber in their heart, they are able to connect with their absolute, divine, flawless imprint that heals and regenerates them in all areas of their being. (In *Light Messages from the Pleiades*, we explained that the sacred chamber in the heart of a human being can best be activated by the frequency of gratitude and by positive thinking without evil intentions.)

This increased frequency connects human beings with higher levels of consciousness. At the same time, thanks to the sacred chamber of the heart, it connects them to their essence, their radiant essence, which in turn connects them to the Divine Source. When human beings find the sacred chamber in their heart, they are connected with their own knowledge, wisdom, and unconditional love for themselves and everything, making them peace-loving and at the same time divine beings.

It is, therefore, essential that as many inhabitants of this planet Earth as possible find their divine essence within themselves and use the ingenious properties of cosmic plasma that will enable them to employ the new healing technologies.

If these technologies were brought to Earth prematurely, the tremendous power they contain could be turned against the population. This is because the many destructive energies existing in the systems of certain beings on this planet would bring havoc and suffering to the population rather than happiness and blessings.

Peace be with you.
Peace be with us.

5

The Power of Words

Use the positive power of your words. Your words are vibrations and waves that are plasmic imprints of your mind. Your thoughts are also plasmic imprints of your mind, every single one. Everything that goes through your mind stays in your personal space. It is not lost "somewhere" in the ether but encoded in your personal reality. What you think is what you are. What you think is what you attract.

***Thoughts are measurable vibrations,
and words are their physical form.***

Words that are positive draw even more positive frequencies into your systems. Words and thoughts create your reality and the actuality of your reality. Words are vibrations that oscillate and attract further frequencies that cause the most varied deeds, situations, or things to materialize. The materialization of your thoughts and words depends directly on the degree of activity of your heart's sacred chamber. The more active this chamber is, the easier it is to form positive energetic imprints.

Each word has its own power, vibration, color, tones, and geometrical forms. Each word is made up of all these magnitudes and all their magical properties.

You can use words to your own advantage and program your personal reality with them. Each word brings a different frequency and a different quality. How loudly you say your words is not important; what matters is how you feel those words when you say them. Your mind expresses itself through your words, and words are the expression of your mind. It is important to realize that your mind (not just your soul) is also a separate being that exists within your system. Your soul, mind, and body form one unit, and your mind is a part of this whole.

Your mind expresses itself through words, and in the past your mind was hurt. Everything your mind has absorbed from its environment is stored in its memory, and now it is time to help your mind to free itself. Your mind (not just your soul) carries its purest essence within, and it wishes to connect to this purest essence and the purity of its heart and soul.

In times gone by, your mind witnessed hugely negative things. It heard, experienced, and perceived words and situations that have weighed heavily on it, which it may still carry in its system.

Your mind, this beautiful being, is longing to be liberated and connected to the purest divine essence at this momentous time. Anything negative it may (still) be sending out to you does not come from its purest essence, but from the accumulated experiences and memories it has been exposed to.

Connect with the beautiful radiant being of your mind, and ask it to forgive you for all the negativity it has had to absorb. Ask forgiveness for everything that has hurt your mind and that negatively affects it to this day.

When we observe the mind of a human being, we often see a being that is still connected in terms of frequency to the negative collective consciousness. We see that the person's light-filled essence is weighed down by the power of the words and thoughts they have absorbed from other human beings. The human mind is, therefore, not able to remember its light and radiant vibration.

Neutralize the vibration of negative words and thoughts that are in your system and are weighing you down. Neutralize the vibrations and oscillations of these words, and begin again. Begin with new words and their vibrations, ones that are consciously positive.

Affirmation to Heal Your Mind

If you wish, you can speak the following affirmation for the healing of your mind:

"Now, and in this space, I contact my mind.

By virtue of my purest intention, I open all the spaces and times of my reality.

I ask my mind for forgiveness for all the negative situations it has had to hear, perceive, and endure in all the times and in all the spaces of my being.

I ask my mind to forgive all those people and beings that have hurt it.

Now, and in this space, with the power and light of divine light and love, I neutralize all the negative words and all the negative thoughts and their vibrations that have settled in my system.

Everything that burdens me and does not belong to my purest essence is dissolving here and now in this divine light."

Now imagine that metallic golden light is streaming to you from the cosmos. It is flowing into your body, illuminating it from the outside and from within. It is also illuminating your aura. The light flows through you and your aura and also into the earth. This light flows continuously, and everything that does not belong to you is channeled into the earth. In the earth, everything negative is dissolved into light.

And now say:

"I bless all the words and all the thoughts that are in my system.

Every word and every thought is healed by the divine light and comes into its divine order in the here and now.

I bless my past.

I bless the purest essence of my spirit.

Divine love, light, gratitude, and blessings fill the essence of my mind.

In the here and now, I encode the vibration of the words 'love,' 'light,' 'gratitude,' and 'blessing' in my system.

Thank you, thank you, thank you."

If you wish, you can now also do an exercise to amplify the love vibration in your system. You can, of course, do this exercise just as well independently of the previous exercise.

Exercise to Amplify the Vibration of Love in Your System

Imagine the word "love" floating in front of your heart. Imagine it in a beautifully radiant color. The word "love" has a rose-gold vibration. You can use this rose-gold, vibrating color, but you can also use another color that you associate with love or that feels to you like the vibration of love.

Imagine more words of love beginning to form, an infinite variety of such words. These words form on their own, all around you. Each word carries its own loving vibration, each letter of the word "love" carries its own intelligence. All these words encode themselves, full of light, in your aura system. They radiate their beautiful vibration into the whole system of your mind, soul, and body (see illustration below).

For positive reprogramming, another method can be used as follows:

Draw yourself as shown in the three pictures. You can also place a photo of yourself on the picture, or you can glue it into the picture (see illustration below).

If you wish, you can place a candle next to the picture so that your intention becomes more visible to the light world. Contemplate the picture each time for as long as you intuitively feel you need to in order to connect and join with the frequency of love.

Of course, you can also use other words, such as the word "protection" (see illustration below).

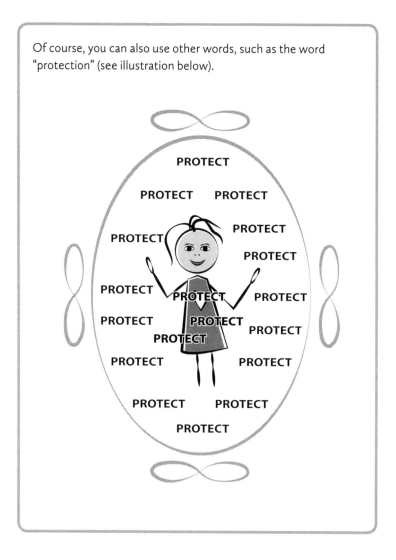

Peace be with you.
Peace be with us.

6

The Here and Now

In a time of global upheaval, almost everyone experiences difficult life situations—situations in daily life, situations in family life, situations in community life, and situations in life worldwide. Almost everyone is pushed to their limits by these situations.

We know that this global upheaval is not easy and often very stressful for you. At the same time, we can observe that the light in the heart of many inhabitants of this planet has been kindled, because these inhabitants have understood the current situation and have realized that low-frequency thinking is dragging them down into low-vibrational levels of everyday life.

These inhabitants of planet Earth have understood that light in their heart and bright thoughts free them from the low-frequency levels of earthly life and lift them up into the light-filled levels of earthly life. They have understood that a light-filled mind and an illuminated heart draw them to positive people, to positive situations, and to everything that is positive in everyday life.

Those of you reading these lines are certainly among these inhabitants, and you know that darkly vibrating thoughts do not get you very far. On the contrary, low-frequency thoughts pull you down into the low-vibrational levels of the third dimension of consciousness that still partially exist on this planet.

Life on this planet is certainly bringing you much joy and happiness in everyday life as well. It is enough to look around, and you will see that this planet offers many moments in which you can experience happiness and joy. Human beings have simply forgotten that the happiness of daily life is what brought them to this planet in the first place. You experience moments, even days, in your life that are extremely joyful and worth celebrating. These moments of happiness in everyday life, however small, are one of the reasons you incarnated on this planet—to experience happiness, no matter how insignificant or imperceptibly small you perceive it to be.

Rejoice in the fact that you are here, that you are alive, that you exist. Rejoice in the fact that you are allowed to dwell in such a perfectly functioning body, one that serves you without you having to make any effort. Rejoice at the sight of flowers, trees, nature, animals, and small children. Live more in the present moment—*in the here and now.*

The present moment connects you with all the gifts arising from what is happening on this planet. The present moment connects you with all the frequencies that surround you. Try to connect your soul and mind with your heart.

In this moment of connection—the here and now—your systems unite. Your heart feels the power of your wholeness; it feels lovingly empowered.

In this moment, it feels like your soul and mind are located in the loving center of your body and your heart can connect with the multidimensionality of your soul. You all know that your soul is multidimensional and its parts are able to spread into the most varied times and spaces of this universe. No matter where they are in time and space or in which loved ones' bodies they exist, all parts of your soul feel connected to you and receive light, love, and healing.

Perhaps parts of your soul are in people with whom you are currently together in your incarnation or part of your incarnation. All the parts of your soul can be healed and illuminated through your personal connection in the present moment.

In the present moment, full of light, you are lovingly connecting with parts of your soul that belong to you. You all influence each other. You are all connected with each other. Everything is connected with everything else.

Everything is connected in love and light. Or should I say, everything *should be* connected in love and light. As a result of the manipulation of the human community and its systems, fissures have opened up both between human beings and within humanity as a whole that prevent energy from circulating freely.

As you know, everything is made of circles, of circular energy, of circular shapes. Everything is interconnected through circles of light. We have often informed you about this fact. Until the human community closes the energy circle and heals the rifts that have created separation among people, it will not be able to ascend collectively to higher dimensions.

In previous texts, we have informed you that the human community is currently undergoing divine healing because the manipulative intervention was too great and the human community would not have succeeded in healing itself in the near future. At this time, the important thing is the ascent to higher levels of consciousness. Planet Earth has already adopted higher frequencies; now it is the turn of the human community.

We know that not everyone has chosen to ascend in the physical body, but in subtle form, everyone will ascend to higher, light-filled levels. In what exact form or shape is of no matter. Some human beings will spend time in the heaven of human beings in order to let their soul be healed by the light rays of the elevated consciousness of other human souls with whom they are connected.

This precise moment in time, the *here and now*, is helping every one of you to meet on the consciousness level in order to contribute to the overall healing of the population. You are all connected to each other on the level of collective consciousness, and all of you influence each other. Let the power of the present moment expand positively into all levels of your existence.

In this moment, in the *here and now*, you not only heal yourself; you also heal parts of your soul and other beings with whom you are connected through your purest essence, and through this you are all connected to each other. All of you are connected simultaneously, both on this planet and in the dimension of what humans call "heaven."

In the moment of the *here and now*, you feel the unity and the magic of the light world. You feel your connection with the light beings, your connection with the Divine Source. You lose your awareness of time, which has often created what you refer to as "stress" on this planet. You feel your connection with all the positive and light-filled frequencies and beings that exist on this planet. The *here and now* connects you with the spaces and times of the cosmic world, which is ordered according to the loving laws and rules of the cosmos.

In this moment, you feel the connection with yourself and your own power flowing through you. You are one, you are whole, you are perfect, you are absolute—just as you are, in this moment. Nothing else matters in this moment—no past, no future, only the *now*, right *here*.

Even these words – the here and now – were programmed by Divine Intelligence to allow you to successfully stay in the present moment and overcome earthly time. In the here and now. Linger in this place, and as often as you can, try to transport yourself to the present moment. Such moments infuse you with life energy and connect you with the cosmic world, where time does not exist.

In this moment you are healing yourself, all the parts of your soul, all your loved ones—basically, all the human beings and souls of the human community, physical and nonphysical. Your light spreads into all times and spaces of your existence. If you like, you can use the following short exercise and affirmation:

Exercise and Affirmation for the Here and Now

First, ask your soul and mind to enter the chamber of your heart, then *repeat the following several times in a row:*

"Here and now. Here and now. Here and now."

Feel the peace that comes to you ("here and now").

Feel the connection with everything radiant and loving ("here and now").

Feel the connection with everything that gives you strength and energy ("here and now").

Feel your own power ("here and now").

Continue, saying:

"Here and now, I am happy."

"Here and now, I am perfect."

"Here and now, I am absolute."

"Here and now, I live my divine being."

These words encode themselves in your system. They also encode themselves in the system of the human collective. Your words help to close the subtle cracks that still exist in the human community.

If you like, you can reshape these affirmations to suit your needs. The words "here and now" carry the divine vibration and help you harness the power of the present moment.

We thank you for your help and for healing not only your system but also the system of humanity.

Peace be with you.
Peace be with us.

7

Orella Speaks about Pavlina and Passes on an Affirmation for a Positive Future

Dear Messengers of Light!

We love you. We love you and have been with you for a few years, thanks to Pavlina. Our Pleiadian family and the members of the Pleiadian Cosmic Council are accompanying you and helping you out of the pureness of our hearts and with the purest intentions.

We specifically engaged with Pavlina and her frequencies in 2011. We saw that she has very pure frequencies and a pure heart. Pavlina chose this task before incarnating into a human body and before incarnating on planet Earth. We appreciate her very much for that, and we protect her. We also protect her family, because we know that the information she brings to the public does not please all the inhabitants of this planet.

We know that the information we transmit enables the peace-loving inhabitants of this planet to understand their overall reality. We also know that the information and frequencies contained in these texts open the hearts of human beings. And the opened human hearts of human beings receive healing cosmic light.

Open human hearts receive the frequencies of the higher light-filled levels of consciousness, even if the person is partially in the third level of consciousness. Now and in this space, with an open heart, you already have access to the positive frequencies of the positive future! Time and space are of no consequence. You have immediate access to these frequencies.

We accompany Pavlina at almost every step and transmit light-filled energies that keep her body, soul, and mind in a heightened consciousness so that she is able to receive light information.

The light of her cells and her inner light are strong, and we value her greatly for that. She is one of us. Just as you, dear readers, are part of us. Many of you who are attracted to our texts and information still carry a part of your Pleiadian soul within.

As Pavlina does. She is part of our community. In fact, she belongs to our Pleiadian family. As a very young Pleiadian girl, she already had healing abilities and helped us heal the members of our families who returned home to us from their incarnation on planet Earth.

She helped them regenerate after all the pain they had experienced on planet Earth. Pavlina's original name, as she told you in one of the texts, is *Siria*. She is connected to the power and healing rays of the sun.

Pavlina also went through a time we call "the time of forgetting." After arriving on this planet, she partially forgot who she truly is. She forgot, as have probably many of you, what great light and what great love she carries within her.

Pavlina has chosen to live through many incarnations here on Earth. She has always helped, she has always healed, and she has always explained the cosmic laws.

The knowledge brought to you in these texts is, in many cases, her own original knowledge, because she herself comes from the Pleiades and only needs to connect to the field of her Pleiadian knowledge.

The knowledge that continuously flows to her is accompanied by our love and light and by information we convey to her.

Many of you are very close to the knowledge in the texts of this book. You feel that you know this knowledge in the depths of your mind. You feel that you have merely forgotten this knowledge. You also carry this knowledge within you. You are all connected.

It is enough to connect to the field of knowledge and remember this information.

We believe that more people will remember in the near future, thanks to Pavlina, who gives the information of the Pleiadian community a physical form. Pavlina has countless light beings around her, guiding her, so that her greatest life task—passing on information—can be manifest and given to Earth's population in physical form.

Light beings are also with each and every one of you. These light beings were called to you through the light frequencies of these texts. They accompany you, they can read your thoughts, and they can connect with your soul. These light beings are in constant contact with your angelic beings, and their common goal is to show you the optimal path for your present earthly incarnation.

Your non-incarnated relatives and friends are also in continuous contact with you and send people into your life who can help you master the most diverse situations on your earthly path. We have already told you several times that each one of you has a whole team of light beings around you. It is enough to be aware of this and to contact them.

The information that Pavlina gives you is of the purest character and is transmitted by virtue of her pure heart. We are already looking forward to meeting her again in physical form and being able to talk about all the things she has experienced here on Earth. We appreciate her commitment to the human community. We know that life in a human body is not easy.

Pavlina is able to communicate with almost all forms within the light world. She is able to communicate with angels, with the non-incarnated, with nature beings, with animals. She is able to instantly decipher our light language, even if she is in a human body. She is able to receive the frequencies and language of the souls of the planets and their beings.

We are happy that she has chosen this task on Earth, and we accompany her as best we can so that she can carry on with her soul task.

We also accompany you, dear readers. Your interest in information connects us and opens the way to you again and again. Everyone who opens their heart is accompanied by our frequencies, and many of you are accompanied by Pleiadian light companions that we send and have already sent to you.

This time is evolutionary and revolutionary in equal measure. Even if many inhabitants of this planet have not yet awakened from their sleep, the development and evolution of humankind is unstoppable. It is already sufficient if you maintain the confidence and conviction that everything is going according to a higher plan, even if it seems to many of you to be the opposite: that the current situation is not positive. Always be aware that you, too, like Pavlina, have come to Earth to help ignite the divine light on this planet.

We belong to one big family. We belong together, and the light in our hearts connects us.

Do not forget your images of your positive future and that of the whole. Visualize and connect to the positive frequencies of the positive future through the power of your hearts.

Call these frequencies to you now—at this time, in this moment.

The positive future is near. It is not far away. It is in the chamber of your heart. You have immediate access to the frequencies of the positive future.

Penetrate the consciousness levels with your intention and ascend to higher, more light-filled levels.

Expand the light of your heart.

Let healing, strengthening frequencies flow into the chamber of your heart through the palms of your hands as well.

Make contact with the angels of the positive future, which are only waiting for your call. They are already at hand. For them, spaces and times are of no consequence.

If you like, you can use the following affirmation to contact the angels of the positive future.

Affirmation: Call to Contact the Angels of the Positive Future

"Here and now, I contact the angels of my positive future.

My pure, enlightened heart connects me with the angels of my positive future.

I ask the angels of my positive future for frequencies and light information that connect me with my positive, light-filled future.

The frequencies and information of my positive future are streaming to me right now.

Space and time are one.

My soul, mind, and body are receiving all the frequencies and light information of my positive future.

The spaces and times of my positive future are permeating my present reality.

The energetic imprints of my positive future are encoding themselves in my present reality in this moment and in this space.

In gratitude I receive all these frequencies and light information.

Thank you, thank you, thank you."

With love!
Orella

Author's Note

And I also thank you all, dear readers! We have been accompanying each other for several years now, since the time the first book in this series was published.

The text Orella has shared surprised me greatly. I had no idea that she would "officially" dedicate her words and gratitude to me in this book. I am much honored, and it is my great pleasure to share this information and knowledge with you. I thank you all for your goodwill and your spiritual light!

8

The Pleiadian Group Members Introduce Themselves

It is now time to lift the veil of mystery. So far, we have communicated on behalf of our community. But now it is time to finally introduce ourselves properly so that you can gain a better understanding of who is communicating with you. We know that having contact with Pleiadian beings is now quite normal for you and that you communicate with us virtually every day. However, there are many human beings who look at this with suspicion and, in some cases, skepticism. We understand that very well. Essentially, the dark beings have manipulated your trust in the good and the light world. After all, the news in your media is still mostly negative.

We think it wise to introduce ourselves now.

So far, five members of our Pleiadian community have communicated with you. Orella is a female being who transmitted the information for the texts. In addition to her, there are four male Pleiadian beings who communicate with you.

After looking at the global situation, members of the Cosmic Council who specialize in passing on these messages joined us.

We were also often joined by the highest member of the Cosmic Council, **ORIN**, whom we value enormously. Orin guides us and instructs us on how best to help the inhabitants of planet Earth. Orin's instructions concern physical help for Earth's inhabitants. We help not only you but also other civilizations—behind the scenes for now and without appearing in public. According to our calculations and our estimation, the time for which we have been waiting for so very long, and which will enable us to make official contact with you, will be here very soon.

Until recently, we four male beings and Orella have been transmitting the texts from our home planet in the Pleiades. Now, our group is in a spaceship close to your planet.

We are not alone here. There are a great many fleets of spaceships in the area that are helping to illuminate planet Earth with light frequencies and light information. In this way, we are helping, with the approval of the Cosmic Council, to increase the consciousness of the inhabitants.

We are protecting planet Earth and its population from attack by negative extraterrestrial civilizations. There is great interest in planet Earth and its population among the negative extraterrestrial civilizations. Firstly, you have minerals and chemical compounds in your atmosphere that extraterrestrial civilizations need to survive. Secondly, both the third level of consciousness and low-vibrational frequencies are still present on planet Earth, providing them with good conditions for their existence on this planet.

But not for long. They know this very well, and that is why they are trying to maintain their hold on planet Earth. At the same time, they feed on the emotions and energies that, thanks to their manipulations, they arouse in the inhabitants of planet Earth.

Our fleets are also located near other planets of your multidimensional solar constellation. There, too, civilizations not unlike that of human beings exist whose stage of development is similar to that of the human community.

Negative extraterrestrial civilizations are also very interested in these planets, which are also just ascending into new dimensions. However, as the populations there manage to withdraw from the low-vibrational dimensions, the dark, physical, extraterrestrial beings will, sooner or later, also have to leave these planets and look for a new dwelling place to meet their parasitic intentions and actions.

In this populated galaxy and its surroundings, planets that are not populated or that vibrate at low frequencies are very difficult to find. In your solar constellation and your galaxy, the percentage of unknown planets that have been newly colonized is extremely small. And, of course, when looking to colonize other stellar or planetary objects, harsh or inhospitable environments for the existence of life as you know it constitute extremely unfavorable conditions.

We protect you, dear ones. We are with you. This is not just an empty phrase. Together with other civilizations favorably disposed toward you, and with the help of human action, we have already succeeded in liberating the inner spaces of your globe, where parasitic races resided in physical form, influencing, in their subtle form, the population on the surface of the earth, human souls, and diverse situations on Earth.

The liberation of the planet is moving forward in exactly the same way that we proceed with you—step by step, and only as much as you can cope with. We are of the opinion that a good-natured human being is in no way able to imagine, even in their worst nightmares, what has been happening inside your planet and, what is more, what has been going on right under your feet, deep below the earth's surface, where utterly unbelievable and terrible things have been taking place.

The planet is beginning to relax because these low-vibrational beings have left it. During our missions, our great advantage is the ability, gained in the course of our evolution, to be able to instantly dissolve our bodies into light-filled energy, which makes us virtually invulnerable. This is our great advantage, and we believe that this advantage will definitely contribute to the liberation of your planet.

We dictate the texts you read here from a spaceship placed near your planet. More precisely, as we are transmitting this information, we are above the prime meridian over Europe. However, we can change our position at any time.

We often return home to the Pleiades and recover from the effects of our efforts. We visit our families, and during the time we spend on the Pleiades, another crew watches over you.

It sounds like your science fiction movies, doesn't it? But believe us, many of the scriptwriters and producers of such films really did have encounters with extraterrestrial civilizations. Some knew about it, and some did not. This is what has enabled them to make films with so much relevant information. Many of their films are very real and correspond to worlds and civilizations as they exist on other planets.

And now we will introduce our Pleiadian group members, as promised:

ORELLA, who communicated with you earlier, is the oldest member of our group. She is related to Pavlina and is responsible for information concerning the healing of the hearts of human beings and information concerning the memory of the purest essence. Her loving information illuminates the systems of human beings.

RAHUL transmits messages concerning the physical state of Earth. He has two small children, a girl and a boy. His wife is active in the background and is connected with him on the consciousness level. She also maintains telepathic contact with him when our group is near planet Earth. (Her name is **ARILLA**.)

MILIN is also a very wise member of our group. He transmits information of a practical nature concerning the development of the human community.

WAHOU is a healer, very well known among us in the Pleiades, who loves to program and transmit number sequences and geometric codes.

Everything concerning healing and healing exercises is in the hands of **RAMUEL**, who passes on huge numbers of healing techniques and practical exercises.

We discuss the different information with each other and then pass it on in a manner that enables Pavlina to receive it in the best possible way. You could say that each of us is responsible for a certain area, but everything we want to convey to you is discussed among us in detail beforehand.

We also work together to prepare information that does not fall within our scope but is still necessary for you to receive. We take turns in transmitting this information.

Another female Pleiadian recently joined us and is now part of our group. She is very gentle, noble, and wise, and we appreciate her very much. She is still young, yet she carries great wisdom and has a deep connection to the cosmic laws. She is also connected with the angelic realm (each of us is accompanied by a guardian angel, just like you) and gives Pavlina information concerning angels and light beings. She has a particularly good connection with the angels of the positive future.

In the texts she will be transmitting to you (she has already transmitted a few), you will be able to feel her enormous, radiant magnitude. Her name is **VILALATA**. This name means something like "the connection of light with matter."

VILALATA will be working with us more intensively than she has been, so our group will now consist of six main members dedicated to transmitting the information you need.

As we have said, we always discuss the necessary topics with each other beforehand and then convey the information in the way that is most helpful to you. You have surely noticed that we transmit information step by step, in a way that can be best understood by human beings.

Before dictating the texts, we connect to a timeline that leads to your human future. In this way, we can discern the phase and stage of development the human community will be going through at the time we publish our information. In this way, information reaches you that is easy for humanity to comprehend. Any information that would exceed the capacity of your understanding right now, we save for later.

We compiled each book in this series in consultation with all our group members and the members of the Cosmic Council. When we had finished compiling the book texts, we contacted Pavlina telepathically so that she knew she could begin writing down our information. Pavlina then connected to the field of each book, which we had prepared nearby. For her, it is like a download.

For us it is always a great honor, because we cannot physically enter your spaces for the time being. But in this way we can help you on your path. We, too, were once in a similar phase of development to the one you are in now. We also experienced manipulation, and we therefore empathize with you. Together with you, we form one big family. We love you.

There are no differences between us. We have similar bodies, we would say almost identical. The only difference is that our bodies have a longer life span. We are slightly taller than you.

We live in communities that help each other. We live out our potentials and our best qualities, those that make us who we are. Each one of us gives back to our family and community whatever it is we can best contribute.

We do not need money. We are capable of materialization. We tend the fruits of nature together. They contain such a high energy value and such high frequencies that eating these fruits is absolutely sufficient for us. But we also make use of light nutrition. This means it is not necessary for us to eat a lot of food to be satiated. And we have such a wide variety of fruits that all our tastes are more than satisfied.

We lead quiet lives focused on our families. We help each other and try to stay in our high light frequency and high heart frequency. This is our great task: to stay in this high light frequency and high heart frequency and not fall back into lower levels. At the same time, it is our great task to help other civilizations in our galaxy that need our support and assistance.

We, too, are in a state of evolution, and by no means do we consider ourselves to be perfect beings. We, too, are working on our perfection.

We are on a good path and have already come a long way. Our hearts are pure. The consciousness work that purified our hearts paid off. We were then able to connect with divine power, love, and energy, and with its intelligence.

We will continue to help and guide you. This is a great honor for us. We value each and every one of you. As you read these texts, your hearts radiate and your body cells vibrate at a light-filled frequency. Your cells rejoice, and you feel connected to us. Your aura shines beautifully as you read.

We can see exactly who is connected to us at any one moment while reading or doing energy work. Your bright radiance connects us immediately—your bright radiance and the beauty of your human heart. For us, every single illuminated human heart is a huge reward for our work. The radiance of your heart is our reward.

We thank you for being. We thank you for the fact that you exist and that you have entered into loving and light-filled contact with us.

Peace be with you.
Peace be with us.
Your Pleiadian Companions

9

Our New Group Member, Vilalata, Transmits Information Concerning the Angelic Realms

I send my warmest greetings to all of you. I greet all souls of goodwill and all those souls who share a bond with me. I am Vilalata. I am the daughter of a very wise Pleiadian scholar and philosopher who initiated me with much kindness into my life task—to convey information about the angelic worlds, the worlds of the light beings, and the worlds to which I have access. The physical human community does not yet have access to these high-vibrating light worlds, but through its evolution it, too, will become mature enough to enter the luminous worlds and dimensions. Every being originated in the divine light, and every being strives toward that light.

The positive future that has already been prepared for the human community is of a subtle nature and full of light. This is what every human being aspires to. What matters is purity of heart and purity of thought. You have been told this many times by my companions. But there is no other way to get there. There is no other path to the light and into the light.

Divine Intelligence has already prepared all of the energetic imprints, color visions, and color worlds for the human community. It is enough to stretch out your arms and connect with these imprints.

It is enough to choose these worlds of light that have already been prepared, using the power of your soul and the power of your mind. It is enough to dive into these worlds, using the power of your soul and the power of your mind. It is so simple. It is enough to control the thoughts in your mind. It is enough to observe your own behavior and to correct everything that does not align with the divine order. It is enough to be aware of it and to apologize—to yourself and others. It is so simple.

The angels of your positive future are working with you. Divine Intelligence has sent them to help you and give you guidance regarding the direction you should take on your life journey. These angels help you to recognize what does not belong to you and does not belong within you, in your inner being—to recognize what does not feel good and what blocks you on your path to happiness.

The angels of the positive future help you to orient yourself in this, currently more than chaotic, world. They help you make decisions that take you in the right direction on your earthly path.

Maybe, even without knowing about these angels, you have had the feeling lately that you intuitively know and sense what is good for you and what is not. You may have noticed a subtle guidance that takes you by the hand and stands behind you as you make your decisions. Perhaps you have felt that someone or something is helping you with your decisions, accompanying you, giving you strength to keep to your decision and not turn away from it. Perhaps you have felt a power within you that you did not know before.

The angels of the positive future come to every human being and connect with the light of their soul. Every human being who has, at least in part, chosen a happy future receives instant help from these beautiful light beings.

These angels know no space and time nor any limits in thinking or perception as human beings do. They move between the spaces and currently existing times of the human community. In earlier times, it was not possible for them to descend into the spaces of existence of the human community because human society was not ready for it. It was not ready for it in terms of frequency.

Now, however, the time has come for the light world to increasingly connect with the human community, providing it with light-filled help—and not only the human community.

These angels have the outstanding ability to work in a light-filled manner with your family in the "heaven of human beings" and with your ancestors. The heaven of human beings has also raised its light frequency and radiant love. It is, therefore, possible for the angels of the future to communicate and work together with your ancestors and family members in heaven.

Your family in heaven and your ancestors have the ability to see into your earthly future. They send people into your life to help you on your way. The angels of the positive future are in contact with them, and together they prepare the best possible path for you. It is enough to become aware of this fact, connect with them, thank them, and show them gratitude.

The angels of the positive future have a truly wonderful appearance. They often enter our space and bring us light-filled information and motivation for the work we do for other civilizations that need help. The angels of the positive future are enchanting subtle beings, whose aura and body shine in the most beautiful colors.

An equally bright future awaits you, if you so choose.

These angelic beings from higher dimensions of light continually visit your earthly dimension to remind you of the higher purpose with which you came here to this planet. You decided to connect with your higher consciousness here on Earth and to subsequently illuminate the earthly reality with your consciousness—not only your own reality but also that of everything that happens on this planet.

In our opinion, you are on a good path, step by step. It is important to stay on this path and not give up. It is important to persevere and not be dissuaded by fake news or false visions. There is already much light and light energy on your planet. Now it is important to take this light into your heart and pass it on. Do not give up on the way. From our higher perspective, we can say that you are close to the goal. Every one of you is important. Every one. Do not pass your responsibility on to others. Take responsibility for your own future yourself. Do not let others act for you. Be active yourself.

Through your actions you create new positive imprints of your positive future. Create as many of them as you can, and enter the new future you have created. No one else can do that for you, only you yourselves. Each one of you carries your future and, at the same time, the future of humanity in your hands.

Enter the new future through the power of your decision, and if you so wish, the angels of the positive future will help you.

With love!
Vilalata

10

Help for Family Members

We know that leaving the third dimension of consciousness demands a lot of strength, especially if your family members have different views and are subject to other social constellations. We feel for you and know that this is not easy.

However, it is important to realize that before coming down to Earth into a human body, you made a decision together concerning this particular incarnation. Many of your family members have chosen frequencies of the manipulative kind. They themselves may still carry certain personal negative elements that they want to process through their stay here on Earth. Nothing happens by chance. Everything proceeds according to previously established arrangements.

If you have the feeling that your family members will accept your help, do not hesitate to explain the current situation to them as it is. Do not hesitate to bless them every day and, in this way, provide them with a portion of divine light and healing for their souls.

Deep within, some family members may be waiting for your help. Perhaps you are one of the people who are here to remind them of their inner light on their journey through life.

Possibly, in the heaven of human beings, you all agreed that you would remind them of their light and the greatness of their soul.

By blessing them every day and sending them the love of your heart, it is possible for them to be reminded of their radiant essence. Do not expect their mind, their thinking, to immediately absorb your help or expect them to reprogram and change their views at an accelerated rate. But believe that the soul of this person will definitely accept your help and encode it in its light-filled matrix. With time, it is possible for the thinking of this person to also change for the better, because the soul passes on its light to the mind.

Some people's minds will accept your help, some people's minds will not. But the soul of these people will always accept your help. The light of their soul will spread farther and farther to the souls of other people. There will be a chain reaction. Through your blessings and light transmissions to others, you contribute to the overall healing of humanity, and sooner or later the field of humanity will be perfectly illuminated.

Just imagine radiant light full of divine love flowing into your crown chakra from the cosmos, flowing on, into your heart, and imagine your heart giving this beautiful light to the person you want to help. Afterwards, bless that person.

In this way, you heal not only others but also yourself, because cosmic light flows through you during the transmission of loving light energy.

Maybe you can help your family members or your loved ones in this way and they will accept your help. Maybe you will soon be able to observe that the person concerned is almost shining already and that their thoughts are beginning to move in a positive direction. Maybe you will be able to observe how the light and blessing that their soul has received is freeing their body from pain or disease.

This very simple but simultaneously very powerful transmission of love and blessing can heal every level of that person's being, for love contains everything that can heal a human being. Love is the most powerful and strongest force there is.

However, there are some people who you can only partially help. Even if their soul registers your help, the person in question may not be able to change their thinking, their views, or their life. Then, it is solely up to them how they live their life during this current incarnation, because they have chosen a different plan or a different life path, even if you may not think it is the best one.

Every person has the right to choose freely, and you must also allow this person to follow the path they think is right. If they have not been able to choose the path of light so far, that has to do with their personal development. Everything strives for perfection, and everything has its rules. Such people cannot overcome obstacles that are much too high for them. They cannot set goals for which they themselves have no concrete ideas or vision. They cannot set out on the path of light if they have to first purify elements in their systems that prevent them from having a concrete vision of the future.

People like this can often only think in shorter time segments. They can only think the way their thinking and their development allows them to, and the way they decided to in this incarnation. Please do not hold it against them. You will save yourself a lot of pain and effort.

If you wish to, you can continue blessing this person, so that they can develop in the best way possible and have more power for their work and deeds here on Earth.

We know it is hard for many of you. We know it is painful for many of you. This time is more turbulent, revolutionary, evolutionary, and significant than any that humankind has ever experienced. It has experienced similar times in the past, but not with such intensity.

Therefore, for many, this phase is a time that demands a lot of strength. In the heaven of human beings, when you were putting together your plans for this incarnation, you had no idea that reality would feel different in the 3D physical world and in a physical body than it did when you were planning your earthly incarnation in the heaven of human beings. In the 3D density, the human being is exposed to many strong frequencies as well as to the thinking of others which can sometimes be cruel.

And that is why we repeat once again the words we have often spoken: We are proud of you, and we value your courage—your courage to be incarnated on this planet at this time; at a time of radical transformation of dimensions and the radical transformation of spaces and times; at a time of radical transformation of evolutionary forms and thought forms and the corresponding 3D matrix rules.

Peace be with you.
Peace be with us.

11

Exercise and Affirmation for Remedying Genetic Manipulation with the Help of the Purest Divine Love

Additional Information Concerning the 4374 Number Sequence

With the following text, we would like to hand over to you information that will help you to neutralize manipulative elements that may be in your physical bodies on the energy level.

The manipulation of the genetics of the human body, which is taking place all over the world at this time, is a well-thought-out deed of huge proportions performed by dark-thinking and dark-acting beings on human beings. We know that this influences not only the mind but also the bodies of human beings.

And we know that you often wonder if it is possible to remove these substances from the body again or to neutralize them.

The purest divine love carries within it all the elements able to help the human being to correct this. Believe us, the purest divine love can neutralize these manipulative genetic substances. This, of course, also requires an internal cleansing of the body. We will talk about that later.

However, the prerequisite for energetic restoration is that the human being in question agrees to the healing and is able, through their pure heart and intention, to receive the purest divine love and its frequency.

It is possible to successfully carry out the correction of the genetic manipulation of the human being because the purest divine holo-gram, which is in the Divine Source, has not yet been interfered with. This manipulation was carried out on planet Earth, but in the Divine Source there are absolutely flawless energetic imprints of every single human being. These absolutely flawless imprints—holograms—cannot be removed from the Divine Source by anyone. And anyone who chooses to restore the health of their physical body and its DNA can heal themselves and return to their original state.

Another important aspect of this healing is that, thanks to cosmic influences, human DNA is connected to new light forms. This means that everyone who is ready for healing can already begin to regenerate their DNA by spending time in nature every day or by spending time in water, for example. They can also contribute to the regeneration of their physical body by drinking high-quality water and through any form of energy work or visualization of light.

The substances that have entered the human body by manipulation do not have to remain there permanently. The duration depends on the light-filled vibration and the consciousness of the human being.

Today, the DNA of your body has the opportunity to reconnect to the light information of the cosmos and the divine order. In earlier times, when human DNA was reduced from the original twelve to just two DNA strands, this manipulation was possible and had a lasting effect because there was not as much cosmic light and divine love on planet Earth then as there is now. Human society existed in lower-vibrational levels of being and living, and it was not possible for it to step out of its heavy state of reality.

Now, however, times have changed and planet Earth is being flooded with light and high-vibration frequencies; therefore, in our opinion, it is possible for human beings to be healed.

As has already been said, this is on condition that the person in question also wants to be healed. Human beings who show no interest in being healed, or who may voluntarily let their body be repeatedly influenced genetically, maintain their free will in this respect.

Another negative aspect of the genetic manipulation you have experienced is that parts of the human soul of the being concerned separated from the human being because they did not feel comfortable in a body manipulated by foreign genetic information. However, these soul parts can be retrieved. They are in dimensional spaces created by the dark beings. This is how they try to gain power over the separated parts of the soul.

In order for the parts of the soul of an affected person to be retrieved, at least three people are needed to form an energetic connection, and these people must have experience with energy work, a heightened consciousness, and a pure heart.

When they combine their forces, they can increase the light energy to such an extent that it becomes possible for them to bring back the lost soul parts into the reality of the person concerned. The retrieved soul parts must then be energetically cleansed and blessed by divine love. For this, it is necessary to ask the soul of the person concerned to take back its parts and thus return to its divine order. We will tell you more about this in the following chapter.

We would like to emphasize here the kindness and love of the light world. We can observe that the separated soul parts of many human beings who have succumbed to genetic manipulation are still held in their light-filled reality. We see that their guardian angels hold and protect these separated soul parts and do not let them enter the artificially created spaces! They hold the separated parts of the soul in their hands and wait for the person concerned to call these parts back and integrate them into their soul.

How noble and loving the conduct of your guardian angels is!

This sight moves us and brings tears to our eyes. We feel and see how the beings of the light world help people wherever they can. And countless people have not the slightest idea that this is happening.

But we do not want to gloss over the seriousness of the situation that so many people find themselves in right now. It is also necessary, of course, to cleanse the body completely of all harmful and polluting substances, especially heavy metals that react to the manipulative substances. Electro-smog and electrical radiation also harm the body even more under these circumstances than when it is in its normal state.

It is important to keep the body in an alkaline, non-acidic state, and to supply it with sufficient minerals and vitamins, especially the C and B vitamins and vitamin D (actually a hormone).

It is also necessary to cleanse the body thoroughly and provide it with all the essential elements it needs. It is best to have your levels tested or checked by an expert so that you can cleanse and regenerate your body in the best way possible. Your natural world also offers you a great number of plants, fruits, and spices that help cleanse and regenerate your body. For example, garlic, onion, and nettle cleanse the blood very well and strengthen the body's immunity.

The Healing, Regeneration, and Protection of DNA through the Number Sequence 4374

In *Light Messages from the Pleiades*, we told you about the number sequence **4374**, which is responsible for the healing, regeneration, and protection of DNA. It was given to you by our companion Wahou, who will support you on the energy level in working with it and your healing process.

This number sequence carries its own intelligence and is connected to morphogenetic fields, which are responsible for the optimal human genetic makeup. It connects you with the absolutely pure imprint of humanity, which exists in the Divine Source.

Your energetic imprints—your holograms—are also in the Divine Source. This number sequence can return your DNA to its original divine state. At the same time, it helps you to eliminate substances from your body that do not belong to you.

This number sequence also has another excellent property. A human being who develops in a very light-filled manner in terms of consciousness can even reconnect missing DNA strands with the help of this number sequence.

Of course, it depends on the purity of your heart, the purity of your thoughts, and on a positive approach to your own body. This number sequence can help tremendously in the development of your light body. The final formation of the light body still lies in the future, but by using this number sequence, you are helping your genetic makeup and DNA to take what may be the first steps toward radiant, illuminated matter. Your cells, in particular, will be happy with this process.

The light information contained in this number sequence, which can help to regenerate, protect, and heal DNA, as well as eliminate harmful substances from your body, brings back the inner light to the cells, which they have, as it were, lost in this low-vibrational body. When the cells in your body light up, and their inner light shines with full divine power again, each cell finds its inner central sun, which carries crystal particles within it. The light of the crystal particles of the individual cells begins to combine so that the crystal networks of your body can form perfectly and you can tune in very well to the crystal networks of Earth and this galaxy.

Many of you already carry crystal networks like these within you. This network runs through your body and connects your meridians with each other. It forms the flowing life force of your meridians. As soon as the luminous connections among your cells have taken place, they integrate by means of their vibration into those crystal networks that your body has already formed. The development of the crystalline systems in your body is extremely important, because these crystalline systems connect you with the universes of your cells and at the same time with the universe where you are at the moment.

Even if the complete development of your light body is still future music for you, you have already taken the first steps. These first steps have come in conjunction with your heightened consciousness, and your heightened consciousness connects you to the higher levels of consciousness.

Step by step, human beings will succeed in amplifying the light of their body and cells. Your pure hearts and pure thoughts will guide you there.

If you need support, use the number sequence **4374** for healing, protection, and regeneration.

There is great power in your human intention. We have observed this many times. Your power of determination is huge and opens all times and all spaces for your healing, for the realization of the most varied matters and for the realization and materialization of your desires and various situations.

If you decide to heal your bodies and ask Divine Intelligence for this with the purest intention, a gradual healing can take place on all levels of your being, step by step, in accordance with the wishes of your body, mind, and soul.

We have prepared an affirmation for you that we have positively programmed in terms of frequency. It is programmed so that your intention and decision to heal is connected in frequency with Divine Intelligence. We have programmed this affirmation so that the vibration of your words connects you to the level of the Divine Source and its love and intelligence. Each of your words is like a vibrating form that connects with the forms of the healing frequencies of the Divine Source.

Exercise with Affirmation for Frequency Healing through Divine Intelligence

First, light a white candle so that you are more visible to the light world, then try to enter into silence. Be aware that you will connect with the loving intelligence of the Divine Source. Through the power of your heart you will connect with the Divine Central Sun.

Proceed as follows:

Breathe deeply and feel the peace in your soul.
Now, let your heart radiate.
Feel gratitude in your heart.

Let a ray of light rise from your heart to the sun in your sky.
After connecting to the sun, let this beam of light continue to rise upward toward the central sun of your galaxy.

After connecting to the central sun of the galaxy, let this ray of light rise higher and higher until you connect to the Divine Central Sun, the Divine Source.

And now, speak out loud:

"Here and now, I connect with the highest and purest love of the Divine Source.

Here and now, my purest intention opens all spaces and times to enable my healing, my regeneration, and the correction of my health condition. The vibration of my words connects me with the highest and purest love of the Divine Source.

Here and now, I ask for the healing of all the systems of my soul.

Here and now, I ask for the healing of all the systems of my mind.

Here and now, I ask for the healing of all the systems of my body.

Here and now, I ask for the healing of all the systems of my energy body.

I allow all the programs and information that do not belong to the systems of my soul, mind, body, and energy body to dissolve in the highest and purest love.

Here and now, my soul, mind, body, and energy body are healed, regenerated, and corrected by the highest and purest divine love.

Healing, regeneration, and correction are taking place right now.

Space and time are one.

Here and now, I ask by virtue of my purest intention for my being to be connected to the purest and absolute, divine energy imprints of my soul, mind, body, and energy body.

These purest and absolute divine imprints come to me in the here and now and merge with all the systems of my being.

Here and now, my soul, mind, body, and energy body are receiving the divine imprints of my perfection.

I ask my soul, mind, body, and energy body to receive these divine imprints and merge with the divine imprints of my absolute perfection.

This reception is taking place right now.
This merging is taking place right now.
I confirm the healing, regeneration, and correction of my
systems.
I confirm my perfection.
The unconditional love of the Divine Source permeates all my
systems.
I am love.
I am light.
I am gratitude.
I am perfection.
4374, 4374, 4374.

Thank you, thank you, thank you."

Now let the ray of light that connects you to the Divine Source separate from it. Watch as your ray of light gently separates and descends toward the central sun of the galaxy. Once there, your ray of light also separates from the central sun of the galaxy, becomes shorter and shorter, and draws back to the sun in your sky. It separates from the earthly sun as well, becomes even shorter, and sinks back into your heart. The light of this ray remains in your heart. Your heart continues to radiate and carry the love of the Divine Source.

For supportive energy healing you can program your water with the number sequence **4374**. To do this, place a glass or carafe of water on this number sequence, let it rest there for at least three minutes, and then drink the water in sips throughout the day as needed.

Peace be with you.
Peace be with us.

12

Retrieval of Lost Soul Parts after Genetic Manipulation

Group Exercise with Affirmation

In the previous texts we told you that, after genetic manipulation, a separation of parts of the human soul took place in many cases.

These separated soul parts can only be brought back into the system when the person concerned is absolutely determined and ready to retrieve these lost soul parts—out of the pureness of their heart, without any egoistic thoughts, in the purest love.

Because love is the most powerful healing element.

This work requires at least three people with pure hearts and elevated consciousness. Assuming three people come together who wish to help the person concerned, the following process can be carried out.

As a supportive measure, apply rose essential oil to the heart region of the person to be healed and also use it in the room where the energy work is to be done. Incense may also be suitable, as well as other supporting aromas, as long as they feel right to everyone involved in this process and no one is allergic to them.

You can, of course, also choose a different process. This is simply our suggestion. The important thing in this process is to stay in a state of love and positive intention, under the protection of the light beings.

Exercise: Retrieving Lost Soul Parts

The person to be healed sits or stands in the center, and the three healers form the points of a triangle around this person. If more healers have come together, they sit or stand in a circle around the person. All participants—the person to be healed as well as the healers—visualize everyone there as standing in their own golden light pillar, which connects them with the universe and Earth.

Everyone then imagines the golden number sequence **8787** in front of their heart. This connects you all with your purest essence and with the purest essence of humanity. At the same time, it protects you with a crystalline, transparent frequency.

The healers interconnect their hearts with a luminous heart ray. After that, each healer connects with the heart of the one to be healed, also with a ray of light.

Everyone now calls upon those light beings that can help them and that they know can support them in this process and at the same time protect them energetically; for example, Archangels Michael, Metatron, Uriel, Gabriel, or Rafael, and the ascended masters, such as Mother Mary and Jesus Christ.

Everyone connects with the power and energy of the Earth and with her soul, Gaia. Everyone can also connect with us, the Pleiadians, if they wish.

All the healers connect with the Higher Self of the person to be healed and with that person's guardian angels.

All the healers connect with the soul, mind, and body intelligence of the person being healed.

Everyone connects to the Divine Source as described in the previous chapter.

Breathe deeply, and feel the peace in your soul. Now let your heart radiate. Feel gratitude in your heart. Let a ray of light rise from your heart to the sun in your sky. After connecting to the sun, let this ray of light continue to rise upward toward the central sun of your galaxy.

After connecting to the central sun of the galaxy, let this ray of light rise higher and higher until you connect to the Divine Central Sun, to the Divine Source.

And now everyone speaks the following words:

"We are absolutely connected with the highest and purest love of the Divine Source.

We ask for help from Divine Intelligence and all the light beings that are now in our space and time. We accept this help with gratitude."

The person to be healed speaks the following words:

"My beloved soul, I (first name of the one to be healed) as well as (first names of the healers) contact you now. In gratitude, in love and in light.

We ask your forgiveness now and in this space and time for the fact that you were hurt.

Please forgive me.

My beloved soul, I now ask for your help.

Connect your light and your love with our light and with our love.

Together we now make contact with your lost soul parts. We now call your lost soul parts back to you.

We ask the highest and purest love of the Divine Source for the purification, healing, and blessing of all your lost soul parts. Now and in this space.

The purification, healing, and blessing of all your lost soul parts is taking place right now.

The integration of all your lost soul parts is taking place right now. In the here and now.

By virtue of our purest intention, we now connect to the Divine Source. We ask the Divine Intelligence to bring back your absolute, holistic, divine hologram into this reality. In the here and now.

Your divine hologram is connecting absolutely with your matrix now and in this space.

The correction is happening right now.
Time and space are one.
8787, 8787, 8787.

Thank you, thank you, thank you."

The healers visualize golden, horizontal eights above the head of the person to be healed, in front of their heart, behind their back in the area of their heart as well as under their feet – four signs of infinity in all. After that, they imagine how these eights begin to rotate in all directions at the same time until they become radiant golden spheres. These radiant golden spheres continue to connect the person being healed with the Divine Source and to protect them. Everyone gives thanks and separates themselves from the Divine Source, as described in the previous chapter.

Now let the ray of light that connects you to the Divine Source separate from it. Watch as your ray of light gently separates and descends toward the central sun of the galaxy. Once there, your ray of light also separates from the central sun of the galaxy, becomes shorter and shorter, and draws back to the sun in your sky. It separates from the earthly sun as well, becomes even shorter, and sinks back into your heart. The light of this ray remains in your heart. Your heart continues to radiate and carry the love of the Divine Source.

The healers watch inwardly as the number sequence **8787** in front of their heart dissolves into golden light. Finally, everyone illuminates everyone else with purple-gold light— their body and their aura.

During the whole process, it is important to take your time between each stage and to feel whether the process has also been successfully completed. You can test whether you have succeeded in retrieving and integrating all of your soul parts using kinesiology, a dowsing rod, or a pendulum. If not, it is important to repeat this process until all of your soul parts have returned.

Should the lost soul parts still be in the care of the guardian angels of the person to be healed, the procedure is much simpler.

You can also test whether these soul parts are with the person's guardian angels. If the soul parts are still with the guardian angels of the person concerned, it is enough for them to contact the guardian angels alone.

In doing so, they can proceed as follows:

The person concerned lets their heart radiate and lets gratitude flow into it.

Light, love, and gratitude connect this person with their guardian angels.

They imagine the number sequence **8787** in gold in front of their heart.

Now the person can say:

"My guardian angels, I connect with you. I thank you from the bottom of my heart for protecting my soul parts.

I thank you for your existence.

I now connect with my soul.

My beloved soul, I ask you to forgive me for allowing you to be hurt.

Please take back your lost parts.

My love and my light protect you.

***8787**, **8787**, **8787**.*

Thank you, thank you, thank you."

Then the person concerned allows this number sequence to dissolve into light in front of their inner eye and illuminates their own being with purple-gold light.

In both cases, act intuitively and with the purest intention and love. The light world and its beings help you during healing processes. And with every healing, you help not only the person concerned, but all of humanity, since you are all connected.

We thank you very much for your light-filled support and send you love.

Your Pleiadian Community

13

Healing the Natural Feminine and Masculine Power

In this message, we would like to teach you a simple technique that will help you reconnect to the natural masculine and feminine power of the cosmic world. In the coming years, the natural state of being of these two elements will help to return your world to its original state—the state it was in when the human community arrived on this planet. This is another step toward your complete liberation on the path to the New Era.

The natural state of being of the masculine and feminine power of the cosmic world is an essential driving force in the healing of this present time. In the past, and still at this time, so many errors have occurred, so much evil, violence, and manipulation has taken place that the human being had to think of and carry out the most diverse tactical steps to be able to survive in this crazy society.

The artificiality of most social contrivances did not allow human beings to live their natural state of being. Men had, and still have, to earn money to support their family. The majority of women became more and more involved in this money-making system because social rules demanded it. Women experienced, and still experience, a dual commitment, being required to play the perfect mother role and the perfect role in their working lives. Many women have submitted to this whim of society and have lost their natural power as a result. Female naturalness has thus lost its magic, its inner power, and its connection to cosmic frequencies.

At the same time, men, from whom absolute commitment in all directions was, and still is, demanded, have lost their connection to the cosmos. The artificially created rules of these artificially created societies have destroyed the inner world and the purest inner needs of every single human being on this planet. The common morphogenetic field of the human community has a lot of energetic "dirt" encoded in it, which needs to be extracted from this field and reprogrammed.

Right now, the energetic correction of the human community is in full swing. The gradual awakening of members of the human community enables more restoration every day. Every human being who comes to the conclusion that they no longer want to live this way, or who changes their mind in the process of awakening, corrects part of their energetic field every day and thereby, simultaneously, also that of the common field, the collective field. In this way, the light of restoration spreads farther into the common morphogenetic field of humanity.

If we look at your collective morphogenetic field from our standpoint, we can observe that each person is playing their own energetic role in this field. When a human being remembers, divine light begins to radiate from their body, and this small light then begins to connect with the collective morphogenetic field of humanity.

At first, the energetic space in the collective field of this person looks like a small luminous star, a tiny point of light in this huge collective field. With every further reminder of the light this person's soul receives, this point, this tiny star, radiates more and more and illuminates and shines beyond the person's energetic field into the collective field. This light expands farther and farther and connects with other lights—the small stars of other human beings. The light of the collective field is directly connected to each one of you. Consequently, its influence on you is direct and unimpeded.

At the same time, although the influence of dark elements and energetic impurities on you is direct and unimpeded, the human community is already on a very good path. An increasing number of people are remembering, and the common field is becoming brighter and brighter.

It is necessary to remember your own natural state of being, your own natural cosmic power and love. Your natural state enables you to find your way back. It enables you to find the way back to your hearts, the way back to your natural state of being, to what makes you human, to people without hypocrisy and without artificially created masks and artificially created behavior and thought forms.

At this time, with the disintegration of artificially created societies that no longer serve anyone, human beings will automatically return to their natural state of being sooner or later. Human beings will understand that mask-wearing and hypocrisies never serve anyone. On the contrary, they are ridiculous and harmful and do not belong in a new world with new levels of consciousness.

Connect as often as you can with the frequency of divine truth, which brings everything back into divine order. Invite the frequency of divine truth into your life, but only when you are ready for it. This is because divine truth is an independent divine power with its own intelligence. Once you decide to work with the frequency of divine truth, you will find that not much of your artificially created reality remains. Your thought system and your life system will be purified by this tremendous power. Artificially created rules, artificially created situations and relationships, and artificially created habits and thoughts will be purified by this power and transformed into divine truth and its purity.

If you begin to work with this driving force, you will see what has been purified in your reality and what kind of artificially created bubble you have been living in. You will see the extent to which your role as a woman or a man has been manipulated on this planet.

You will also see how your relationships are purified—not only those within your family but all kinds of relationships. In all likelihood, you will all experience intense purifying situations, but these situations bring clarity and purity to your relationships and clarity and purity to you, too.

The frequency of divine truth has already begun to flow to planet Earth. Step by step, it is purifying the systems that need purifying first. Divine truth helps you purify and clear those systems that do not have a pure vibration. At the same time, it helps you create systems based on truth, purity, and honesty.

This process will not just take a few weeks or months. You will have to exercise patience and find strength within yourselves for a few more years. The manipulation on this planet has affected almost every system; however, if you are ready for it, you can expect a positive, pure, and truthful future—not only in terms of the future of the community but also in terms of your personal future.

And now we come to the promised exercise that will help you reconnect to the natural cosmic feminine and masculine power. It is very simple. Through this exercise, you will reawaken the natural state of being within you and in so doing, purify yourself of the energetic burdens of past incarnations you have lived through on Earth in the role of a woman or a man.

Exercise to Connect to the Cosmic Feminine and Masculine Power

Breathe deeply, in and out.

Sit or lie down, and keep your spine straight.

First, activate your hands. To do this, turn your palms upward and imagine pink light flowing to one hand and light-blue light flowing to the other.

Then say:
"The chakras of my hands are activated by the natural cosmic feminine and masculine power. My intention is pure and clear.
The chakras of my hands are activated now and in this space."

Now place both hands on your sacral chakra. Let the colored frequencies that flow through your palms flow into your sacral chakra.

And now say:
"I forgive all people and all beings who have violated my natural feminine and masculine power.

I forgive myself in all the times and spaces of my whole existence.

My forgiveness is absolute.

Here and now, with the power of cosmic light, I heal all the burdening emotions, memories, and thought patterns that I have experienced here on Earth as a man and as a woman.

My sacral chakra is being healed here and now.

Here and now, through the power of cosmic light, all emotions, memories, and thought patterns that do not belong to me are being transformed.

Now and in this space, I connect to my natural state of being.

Now and in this space, I connect to my natural vitality and energy.

Now and in this space, I activate my healing.

Now and in this space, I bless my natural state of being, vitality, and energy.

I am perfect.

I am pure.

Thank you, thank you, thank you."

Through this energy work, and especially through your intention to return to your natural state of being, your DNA will also begin to heal, purify, and regenerate. The genetic information that makes you a woman or a man will begin to come back to you. You will return to your perfection and natural state of being, step by step.

In this way, you are simultaneously helping to heal the natural state of being of your ancestors of both the female and male lineages.

We thank you for your work.

Peace be with you.
Peace be with us.

14

The Positive Power of the Collective Field of Humanity and Communication with Animals

I, Vilalata, am speaking to you. It is a special honor and a great pleasure for me to speak to you and communicate with you. This new time brings with it great changes in human thinking. You people of goodwill know where the path on this planet is leading.

I often look at this situation and discuss it with my Pleiadian companions, and we observe what is happening on the planet. We know that many of your human companions feel distressed and many of them have begun to complain about their fate and the injustices of the situation. Many of them even condemn the light world and have lost hope in the future. Many of them have closed their eyes and gone back into the dark clouds of the dark reality. It is a pity that they have not successfully managed the life test they planned for this incarnation—the test to remain true to themselves, the test to remain true to the light world—*to the light world, which is home to all of you.*

A similar situation has already occurred several times on Earth. Human beings have, in the past, decided on several occasions to take what is perhaps—and we would like to emphasize this—the greatest and most daring of all tests, the test to lovingly remain true to oneself. But even if they did not successfully manage the life test, these human beings made a great deal of progress nevertheless, and gained further experience for their next incarnations.

We should not judge, none of you and none of us. Our common task is to accept the decisions of others, even if this acceptance is often painful and disappointing.

I, Vilalata, now bring you words of hope, peace, and joy. With these words, I am transmitting frequencies of positivity to you that you can use for this time and the next. And I am not alone in transmitting them to you, my Pleiadian companions are, too. The angels that are responsible for this planet and for the development of the human community are also transmitting them to you right now.

We know that loving frequencies are necessary in every moment of what is happening here on Earth. We know that many people often feel themselves to be alone. But we also know that, in the depths of their soul, every human being senses that the support of the light world is there. Those of you who have decided in this incarnation to move toward the light receive enormous light-filled help every day. The more of you there are, the more the hearts of each one of you and your whole system shines.

You are full of light—and the light connects you with each other. You support each other!

You are surely able to feel that at certain moments an enormous power flows to you, which drives you on in a positive way. Perhaps you sometimes wonder where this power comes from. At such moments, you are experiencing a powerful connection with the collective of human beings who nurture the exact same decision for a positive future as you. They carry light within them, the light of their heart, which has drawn to them a vast number of light beings and light frequencies. This luminous force has the ability to multiply and expand into all times and spaces of your common human existence.

And the light-filled power of the collective is becoming stronger and more forceful in its positivity. Each one of you contributes to this collective power through your work.

At those moments, when you feel this tremendous power within you, you are connected to the positive power of the collective and to the power of the light world. The more of you there are, the more intensely you will feel the power within you. This power will accompany you in your earthly body through your earthly life. You will feel a power that you have never known before in your earthly body.

Consciously allow this motivating, tremendous, luminous force to flow into your systems and into your hearts. You are also supporting the members of your family and your human colleagues who, in the depths of their souls, have chosen the same path as you and have just not had the strength to allow this powerful light and energy to flow into their system.

Through doing this, you likewise support members of your family and your human colleagues who decided to go a different way, because the purest essence of their soul accepts your light and thereby receives light impulses and light information for their further development.

Although their thinking is moving in a different direction, a part of their soul receives your light and, sooner or later, will remember that light—maybe not in this incarnation but in their next incarnations.

You are all connected with each other. You are connected to the purest divine essence, which all of you carry within, without exception, even those people of whom you might believe the opposite. Every person carries the purest divine essence within them, and every one of you will remember it at some point. Earthly time is of no importance. Time does not matter. At some point, the memory will come.

Support from Light-Filled Nature Beings

During this time, you will also receive great support from light-filled nature beings—more than ever before. Light-filled nature beings bind you to nature and its kingdoms. They connect you to the realm of minerals, plants, animals, and all natural elements. They connect you to the realm of benevolent insects that help you recognize the subtle vibrations within you.

Each kingdom of nature plays a specific role, and each kingdom of nature supports you on your path to light and freedom. You surely already sense an increased connection to nature and its beings, living and non-living. You sense that nature makes you happy and joyful and brings back your physical and mental health. Animals are communicating with you more and more effectively. You may sense that not only are your pets communicating with you but also other wild animals.

The communication coming to you from these animals has not changed. These animals have also communicated with you in the past, but human beings are now reaching the stage where they are able to receive and understand the language of animals.

The purity of your heart is increasing your connection with animals and will continue to connect you even more through the purity of your heart and the purity of your thoughts. The more you regain your purity of heart and mind, the better you will be able to tune in and understand the animals around you.

We know that many of you have been communicating with the animal kingdom for a long time, but even those of you who are already successfully communicating with animals will have an even better and more focused connection with them and understanding of them in the future.

Animals send out their waves of consciousness to you, and you are now well able to receive them.

You are connected to their field of consciousness. The development of your consciousness enables you to do this. The more of your accumulated negativities and burdens you let go of, the easier it will be for you to communicate with animals and the kingdom of nature. You will also be able to understand plants and minerals and other beings.

Your mind is freeing itself and successfully rising above the low-frequency 3D levels. The liberation of your mind and the purity of your heart are enabling you to communicate with and understand the animal kingdom and all the kingdoms of nature. The purity of your mind and the purity of your heart are connecting with your body. Your body will also radiate purity and love. Animals will lose their fear of you. They will sense the purity and love that emanates from you. They will deliberately connect with you.

This connection with the animal and nature kingdom will also help you, step by step, to move toward your radiant future. Looking into the eyes of an animal connects you to the purity and consciousness of the animal world—a world without negative thoughts and without condemnation, a world of love for oneself and connection to light-filled nature beings.

People will move into their radiant future accompanied by light-filled nature beings, each mutually strengthening the other. Their fellowship and common love will heal the fields of those animals that have been hurt. They will heal the energetic systems of the animals, which, due to their suffering, became caught in an intermediate dimension between Earth and the heaven of the animals and were not able to ascend any higher.

Their common love will free the animals from these intermediate dimensions. The consciousness of human beings and the consciousness of animals will be liberated. The souls of the animals that are still in these intermediate dimensions will feel immediate alleviation and will rise out of this intermediate "prison." The souls of these animals will connect with their divine power and divine origin, with the origin of their natural state of being.

Your love for nature and all its beings is liberating humanity, step by step, from the low-frequency levels of your common existence. Do not forget that at this time everything will go more quickly and easily. Your intention now has greater power and greater potential for manifestation than before. Love for yourselves liberates your existence here on Earth. You are connected. You are connected with each other. You influence each other.

Find complete love for yourself and accept the help of the animal beings who started to communicate with you long ago. Your love for yourself and your purity of heart and mind will connect you.

Your
Vilalata

15

Cosmic Healing Tones and the Essence of Your Soul

In the previous text, we could feel the beauty of the words that connect you with the love and natural state of being of the animals. Your love for your pets and animal beings will become stronger and more meaningful. Your love for animals and animal beings heightens your senses for everything that is essential—not only your love of animals but also your love of nature and all its elements.

Now I, Orella, am speaking to you.

I am watching the light of your hearts.

With each passing day, the light of your hearts is increasing and becoming more beautiful and radiant. Every day on this planet is another step along your path to the light, to the light of your soul and the light of your existence.

The light of your soul is your essence. You have come to this planet to live your essence. There is no other path to the light than the path of light. Light contains all the elements and carries everything your soul needs and longs for. The light of your soul is not only connected with the cosmic light but your soul encodes and stores this cosmic light in itself continuously.

Your soul knew before entering your physical body that there would be enough light for its growth exactly at this time on this planet. That is why it entered your physical body.

The powerful cosmic light falling on your planet contains all the elements of the cosmos. It contains not only frequencies, vibrations, colors, and geometrical forms but also sounds and tones that connect with everything living and non-living that exists on this planet.

The cosmic tones contained in the cosmic light can best be absorbed by your body when your whole system is in a calm state. You can absorb the sounds of the cosmos best when you are in the silence of your soul and in the silence of your mind, even if this sounds paradoxical.

You can best absorb these healing cosmic tones when your soul and spirit have become calm and have found peace within themselves. The stillness you experience in deep meditation, for example, connects you to the stillness of the universe, which at the same time is full of healing tones that heal your overall system.

In deep meditation, at the point when your senses flow together and you perceive them as one unified state, I'm sure that you have noticed that you stop perceiving sounds and what is happening outside. Your mind then connects with your body and soul as one in unity consciousness. Your whole system, formed by this unity, connects with the silence of the universe. Nevertheless, an incredible number of sounds exist in the silence of the universe, which human beings do not hear, but which they feel.

Your soul, mind, and body feel them.

You have surely experienced a situation when you felt ill or out of sorts and felt like withdrawing from the outside world and the people around you, when you wanted to hole up and be alone. In this "first aid" moment, your self-protective mechanism forced you to take the time to unify mind, body, soul, thereby connecting them to the healing power of the silence of the universe.

At this moment, your soul, mind, and body system receives healing units of cosmic healing tones, which connect with the consciousness of your cells and especially with your blood and with all your body fluids, which then pick up the vibration of the tones and vibrate in their rhythm.

The tones of the cosmos streaming to you look like beautiful radiant sparks pulsing with light and connecting with your system. It is a wonderful spectacle. Each cosmic tone has a different color and a different healing property. The tones create beautiful geometrical forms in your systems that, full of light, interconnect and create a magnificent, luminous symphony. It looks as if these luminous structures that connect with each other are dancing, full of light, through your body, connecting with the symphony of the universe at the same time.

Your non-incarnated family in the heaven of human beings can certainly tell you about this wonderful gift from the Divine Source. Your family, who are in the light, experience and perceive these lovely symphonies.

Multiple light-filled spaces exist on the level of the heaven of human beings. Multiple light-filled spaces exist on the level of the Divine Source. Every single space is characterized by a different cosmic tone or interplay of tones that heal and transmit the frequencies of peace, happiness, and joy to human souls.

Cosmic tones, characterized by their magical subtlety, allow the soul to experience its radiant essence and spread its light and beauty into all the spaces of its being.

There are different tone spaces into which human souls enter and in which they can let their experiences from their earthly incarnations be healed. Every human soul can choose which spaces it enters and which issues are to be healed. Even souls that have already been completely healed enter these spaces because the cosmic tones cause their light to expand.

Light-filled spaces also exist where there are no tones, because in the world of cosmic divine happening there is nothing that does not exist.

Human souls can choose the spaces they find pleasant for simply being in and for their healing and to which they feel attracted on the vibrational level. When meditating in your earthly world, you are connected to these spaces as well. You are connected to the magic and healing power of cosmic tones. Beautiful, luminous sparks of cosmic tones dance in your body and rejoice and give you energy and health, even if your perception cannot grasp their sound.

In the future, healing with cosmic tones, which you are not yet able to perceive consciously, will be one of the main ways to help heal the systems of the human body, soul, and mind. The light-filled energy that will heal you—thanks to new technologies—is able to convey the power of cosmic tones and their plasmatic, colorful, divine imprints to your systems.

As I have already told you, a wide range of elements in light are available to heal your whole system. The new technologies that have already been prepared for the human community allow human beings to connect to their perfect divine hologram and, moreover, to connect to cosmic spaces containing the most diverse healing tones and frequencies.

Your soul very much enjoys every meeting with the sounds of the cosmos, because it was able to perceive these sounds when it was in the realms of light. The light and all its frequencies and elements are its essence.

Your corporeal sheath also yearns to reconnect, and your DNA is also able to instantly connect to these cosmic tones.

The best connection of your DNA to cosmic tones happens during meditation or when you feel happiness and joy and your light-filled vibration increases as a result. Through this, your DNA, especially when you are in nature, is capable of regenerating itself by reconnecting to cosmic tones and every frequency of light. But we have already talked about that several times.

Simple yet huge possibilities for healing await you. The more you learn to consciously experience moments in which there is a deep connection of your spirit and soul with your body, the more healing and light-filled information from the cosmos will flow to you.

In time, you will feel that you are becoming an integral part of the cosmos and of the whole. You will feel that your connection with the cosmos is your essence. You will feel that the light and all its qualities are your essence, and you will perceive that you yourself are a radiant essence.

The more you connect with the systems of your soul, mind, and body, the more you will find your self-healing powers to be more than active and will be able to verify that you are your own healer. You will feel your own strength and positive power. The light connects you with everything fundamental and essential. You yourselves have come from the light and have brought light to this planet. You yourselves are part of the divine light, for it is within your soul. The divine light in your soul makes you what you are: a human being with a radiant core.

You are returning to your divinity, step by step. Many of you have already come a long way and discovered the divine light within you. Some of your human companions have forgotten this light. *But that, too, is part of the overall reality of humanity.*

Those of you who are aware that you carry the divine light within you have surely found that the Divine Source is not "somewhere very far away," but right there in your hearts.

Between you and the Divine Source there are no boundaries and no hindrances. The hurdles and limitations are only in your mind. Your heart and soul have already recognized this fact and are encouraging you to meditate regularly, to connect your soul and mind to your body regularly, and they are trying to connect you again and again to moments in which you experience happiness and joy.

Your soul and its light continually connect you with everything divine, with everything fundamental, and with everything essential. This law of light and the striving toward the light cannot be denied or circumvented in any way. Striving toward the light is part of your light-filled evolution. This evolution is unstoppable and inevitable.

Although some dark beings and powers act to try and stop your light-filled evolution, they cannot succeed, because following the path to the light is your soul's greatest desire, and this wish is heeded by Divine Intelligence.

In this current phase, in this space and time, a light-filled evolution and progression toward the light is dawning. This is part of the development of the human soul and human development as a whole. Everything strives toward light and love. There is no other way.

The human community has already embarked on this path. The human community is already on its inexorable way to the light.

This is a magical and mystical time—a time when your soul is experiencing its most rapid spiritual surge ever. From a cosmic point of view, your soul is experiencing the greatest thrust toward the light it has known. It is our honor to accompany you during this process through light-filled means.

With love!
Orella

16

Ramuel and His Information on the Transmission of Healing Energy on Mondays

Greetings, I am Ramuel. I greet you and, along with my greetings, I bring the wave of healing energy that will help your heart to specifically receive the vibrations of cosmic love.

Your bodies are receiving the frequency of cosmic regeneration at this time and are beginning to adapt excellently to the new vibrations from the cosmos that your planet is receiving. This type of regenerative healing now flowing to you is bringing you unique and high-vibrational light information that your body has not yet experienced during your incarnation so far.

Your body is simultaneously adapting to the new, light-filled vibrations, and the information coming to you from the sun.

The interplay of vibrating frequencies that your body is experiencing can make you feel tired or exhausted. On the other hand, it sometimes brings you joyful euphoria. Your sleep may also be affected by these cosmic events. You may need more sleep. You may have been having trouble sleeping lately. Your body does not absorb information from the sun during the night hours; it absorbs information from the cosmos.

During the night hours, your body's system adjusts to the frequencies of cosmic healing. Throughout the day, your system absorbs information from the sun and information from colors, which mainly influence your hormonal system. At night, light information comes to you that regenerates your body.

Your body is going through an extreme phase at this time, because the light information that your body is taking in is affecting all of your body's systems.

The bodies of human beings are becoming subtle. They are beginning to tune in to the frequency of the cosmos, and they struggle on a daily basis with the extreme conditions that still exist on your planet. They fight pollutants that are in your food, and they fight pollutants that are in the minds of human beings.

Your bodies need rest and good nutrition and water during this time of transition into new, high-vibrational levels. Your bodies need houses without electrosmog, because electrosmog is now harming your subtle body more than before.

Your bodies need nature. *In nature, they are given the opportunity to attune themselves to the unity of the cosmos.*

Your healing and the progress of your healing are enormous at this time. The healing processes for body, soul, and mind have covered the first stretch toward more subtlety through, what you might call, seven-mile steps. The transformation of negativities has helped you to develop the regenerative abilities of your body.

Even though you are dealing with the complexity of the overall situation at this time, your bodies are going through a process of healing, regeneration, and renewal of individual systems.

Those of you who have chosen to focus on purifying your body will observe that your entire being is growing more subtle and, increasingly, your body has an improved ability to connect with your soul and mind. You will observe that your systems are capable of instantaneous connection with each other at all times and not just during meditative states. You will observe that you can better understand the nature of your soul, the nature of your mind, and the nature of your body.

What Happens during Monday Meditations

Dear supporter of our Pleiadian information,

Thanks to Pavlina, I have been accompanying you for several years. During evening sessions every Monday, from 9 p.m. to 9:20 p.m. local time, I work with every one of you, observing you and reviewing the work you have done to heal your systems. Your mere intention connects me with you. I am not the only one that works with you. A large number of Pleiadian beings—both physical and those that exist mainly in their luminous form—are there, too. We are able to work with you in *the moment*—no boundaries among dimensions, spaces, and times. Those of you who choose this targeted healing immediately receives a whole range of healing frequencies that are beneficial not only to the body but also to the soul and consciousness of the human being.

The transmission of healing frequencies comes to you the moment you make this choice, not only during the Monday transmissions. During the Monday transmissions, however, you will receive additional, enhanced healing, as thousands of representatives of our Pleiadian frequencies consciously, through light-filled means, strengthen the entire healing field and its vibrations.

During this transmission every Monday, which usually lasts no more than 20 minutes of your earthly time, we have ample time to heal and regenerate all parts of your systems.

During this 20-minute transmission, other light beings come to you. Your cosmic families and your non-incarnated relatives and ancestors also come to you, wishing to help you right now and convey information. Your light helpers transmit healing, energetic purification, and regeneration and raise your consciousness through light information.

For me and for all the other Pleiadians and radiant beings that work intensively with you, these 20 earthly minutes are a very moving and thoroughly positive emotional event of great depth.

Watching you in the presence of these radiant beings and frequencies is such a beautiful sight that it moves us to tears every time. Observing how many of you sit down regularly for these energetic transmissions and how many of you have already succeeded in entering the phase of subtlety of body, soul, and mind is simply indescribably beautiful.

You may not be aware that this transmission also works with the souls and the consciousness of your individual organs. It works with the consciousness of your individual body systems. You may not be aware that your cells are picking up these colored light vibrations and encoding them into their systems. Every cell of your body is preparing to activate, sooner or later, the inner crystal sun within itself, which, through its absolute activation, will connect you to the crystalline structures of your galaxy and your Earth. During the regular, light-filled transmissions of cosmic information, your cells raise their vibration and receive impulses they have long awaited.

During these powerful, light-filled transmissions, your guardian angels are also full of joy, because they are also in the light—and not only in the light being transmitted to you but also in the light of your heart. Your guardian angels see your heart's light, connect with you directly, and provide you with light-filled assistance for the next days of your earthly life.

Your light attracts a countless number of other luminous vibrations and entities.

Your guardian angels are always happy when your system radiates. They then have much easier access to you. They can connect with the emotions of your soul and with the thoughts of your mind. They can connect with the intelligence of your body. They can sense what you need for your earthly path and can call specific other light beings or your ancestors to you, who can support and help you in the individual areas of your being.

You may not be aware that your light increases tremendously during the Monday transmissions, and that you automatically give this light to those around you and to your families and loved ones that you might be staying with right now. I see that your light intensity and light protection continue for several days, depending on the situation, constitution, or environment you are in. I see that each of you is still in your personal sphere of light, which continues to nourish, regenerate, and protect you energetically in a light-filled manner for some time.

Your consciousness increases with each energy transmission— with each energy transmission and each time you do energy work, not only during the Monday transmission. Your consciousness vibrates in beautiful rainbow colors and connects you instantly—without boundaries in space and time—with the rainbow colors of the levels of consciousness toward which the human being is currently striving.

During the energy transmissions every Monday, subtle portals are created in your immediate vicinity through which negativities that are currently leaving your systems are discharged. These subtle portals direct the excreted negativities into previously created dimensions, so that they can be dissolved into light in those dimensions and no longer burden your homes and the rooms during the energy transmission.

We and the light beings create a healing space for each one of you individually, regardless of where you are physically located at any particular moment.

Everything is well thought through, and with the help of the light world and its beings, everything is possible and feasible. We work with you in the way your overall system desires.

We help and support you in your process.

During the transmissions every Monday, your intuitive and telepathic awareness also increases. Your healing abilities and self-healing powers improve. Your potentials and your creativity are strengthened. This is because the intensity of your heart light connects you with the light of the Divine Source, which is your home and where all your potentials and abilities and all your holographic, flawless, energetic imprints are located.

During these transmissions you can, of course, communicate with us. Your mere intention already connects you with us. Your intention also connects you to your light companions, which are near you. If it is in accordance with your divine plan, you are helped on the most diverse levels of your earthly incarnation.

In the Monday transmission, you can use the number sequence **3717** that my close and warm-hearted companion Wahou has given you. This number sequence connects you more strongly with us. It opens your spaces and times and connects you to our spaces and times. You will then become more visible to us, the Pleiadian beings.

The digits of this number sequence have their specific vibration and intelligence. They raise your consciousness and your ability to connect with us. At the same time, they carry the frequency of confidence that helps you to stay in your power and maintain confidence in this phase of the societal situation. They fill your hearts with confidence and with understanding of the higher purpose and meaning of this global phase.

You are welcome to transfer this number sequence to water and drink it in sips. You can also write it on a piece of paper and keep it near you. You can look at it or say it out loud. This sequence of numbers connects you with us and also provides you with energetic protection from any negative energies, beings, or people.

Before and after Receiving the Pleiadian Healing Energy

If you wish, you can speak an affirmation before the energy transfer. You can also use this affirmation with other energy transmissions we offer.

Say aloud:

*"**3717, 3717, 3717***

Here and now, I open the spaces and times for receiving healing energy and information from my Pleiadian and light-filled companions.

Through the power of my intention, I connect with all the loving light frequencies and light beings that can give me the energy of healing, regeneration, protection, and consciousness development in the here and now.

I receive all positive, light-filled, and loving energies with gratitude.

Now, and in this space, time and space are one.

Thank you, thank you, thank you."

After the transmission, take some time for yourself so that the new frequencies that heal your system can successfully connect with your system. Drink enough water so that your body can eliminate all the toxins that have settled in it and in your mind and psyche.

On behalf of the entire light-filled team, I thank you from the depths of my heart for the work you are doing. Your work on yourself also illuminates the systems of other human beings and the systems of the collective field of humanity.

Your
Ramuel

17

Your Pleiadian Soul Part, Its Journeys through Time and Space, and the New Number Sequence of Remembering

Sharing information gives us great pleasure. We love to transmit information and light-filled healing frequencies to you. We have been accompanying you for so long, every one of you. Certainly, for considerably longer than you think.

Many of you carry a soul part of the Pleiadian civilization. Many of you also carry a part of the Pleiadian energy. And this Pleiadian soul part and the Pleiadian energy connect us with each other.

We are convinced that all of you who study our information and work with our healing techniques carry components of the Pleiadian civilization within you. Otherwise, you would not be attracted to our information and to the Pleiadian energy.

This is true for everyone—you, included.

If you feel love, connection, and attraction while reading our texts, you can be sure that a part of your soul holds a Pleiadian aspect or essence. This soul part has led you to the information you are reading here. It has brought into your life people who have led you to this energy or information.

Perhaps you are also one of those people who feel a deep longing inside them when they look at the starry sky—the longing to return to the Pleiades star cluster someday. Every one of you who feels energetically attracted to us is not here on planet Earth by chance.

Even as you process certain matters related to your human core, the Pleiadian soul part in you has brought you to Earth for an entirely different reason. Your Pleiadian soul part has come to this planet with a different purpose: *to help the human community at this time of transition to higher dimensions.*

People with a Pleiadian soul part were originally healers. We, too, love to heal and convey information that pertains to healing. Every one of you who is attracted to our texts carries healing abilities within you. Many of you have already discovered them; many others of you suspect that you carry them within you and long for their activation.

Healing is our most important innate ability, and at the same time, healing is the task given to us by Divine Intelligence. You could say that healing the systems of body, soul, and mind is what distinguishes us the most—not only healing the systems of body, soul, and mind but also healing nature and the most diverse areas of life.

Another great task for which we live is to help others—to help *all those* who are in some kind of stressful life situation, to help *all those* who have been wronged.

We carry within us a strong sense of justice. We carry within us a deep compassion for others, for all beings, living and non-living. Perhaps you are also people who long for justice. Maybe you are also among those people who experience great joy and happiness in helping others.

Your Pleiadian soul part guides you through this earthly incarnation and gives you indications as to how you can live in the best and most meaningful way. Your Pleiadian soul part connects you with us. You may often feel the need to help and to share your healing abilities. Your Pleiadian soul part guides you along this path and interlinks you with other people who also have a Pleiadian soul part. The essence of your Pleiadian soul part connects you with each other. On this planet there are a large number of people who have a Pleiadian soul part. A huge number of people have chosen to work on this planet during this time.

You are not here by chance.

Perhaps your life has seemed incomplete until recently. Perhaps your life has seemed meaningless to you until recently. However, at this time, this evolutionary and revolutionary time, you have been led to a stage in your life where you know with complete certainty why you are here. It is absolutely clear to you that this is what your Pleiadian soul part wanted. You are among those people who manage to change their environment positively with their energy, light, and love. You succeed in positively influencing the people around you.

During this time, an energetic activation of your Pleiadian essence is taking place. Divine Intelligence has activated all those soul parts in human beings that are of extraterrestrial, peace-loving character, and origin—not only the Pleiadian soul parts but also the soul parts of other peace-loving civilizations in people of goodwill.

At this time, Divine Intelligence has activated all the soul essences of extraterrestrial, peace-loving origin that are in human beings. The divine light that passed through human souls has activated the memory of why they really came to this planet.

It has activated the memory of their task and their healing abilities. It has activated the memory of the cosmic love they carry within them.

The light-filled frequency of the soul essences of extraterrestrial origin connect with each other at this time and create a subtle, luminous structure among human beings. Know that about one-third of the population of this planet carries a Pleiadian soul part. All of these people are increasingly contributing to the overall ascent. And this multitude, of course, includes children who have come to this planet with their higher purpose.

Even if some people do not yet remember precisely and consciously the task of their Pleiadian essence, the activated light of their Pleiadian soul part and their Pleiadian energy is already bringing subtle frequencies to this planet and helping others in this way.

Many of you have been manipulated in previous incarnations. The dark forces have done everything to extinguish your Pleiadian light and not allow it to connect with the light of other peace-loving people and with the light of the Divine Source. This manipulation was targeted. To this day, it is continuing with the same aim.

But all of you foresee that the final departure of the dark beings and powers from planet Earth is only a matter of time, and we can confirm that.

The awakening of humanity and the human being's remembering of their own light and love of their heart is proceeding rapidly.

Everything that is cosmically related helps in this process.

The Connection of Your
Soul Parts during Sleep

At this time, the connection of the Pleiadian soul parts is enhanced during sleep. While your body sleeps, a part of your soul emerges from your physical matter into dimensions, spaces, and times where it meets with other souls. They unite their light. They combine their best features and support each other. Every time they interconnect in this way, they are granted further activation by the divine light. They receive impulses from the Divine Source and encode information in themselves that is needed at this time for personal growth and for the growth of healing abilities. Having formed this connection, the Pleiadian soul parts move together into dimensions, spaces, and times in which they can pursue their task of helping the whole human society or individual human communities. The Pleiadian soul parts combine their abilities, their light, and their love and help in dimensions, spaces, and times where this is needed.

For many of you, your Pleiadian soul parts enter the past, present, and future of human society during sleep. Together with other souls, you are then able, for example, to change certain events in the past so that what happens in the future of humankind is positive. You are capable of such actions. You are capable of reprogramming negative events that have been encoded in the field of humanity's future by the dark forces of the past.

This ability will increase. But even now, at this moment in time, through your intention and the purity of your soul, you are able to reprogram negative situations in the future as part of the collective light work that takes place while your body sleeps, in all times and spaces. You are able to enter into the most diverse dimensional spaces where you can decipher or decode certain situations that would negatively affect the future of humanity.

You enter these dimensional spaces and times through your light chakras, which are located above your head. These chakras are gateways and portals to parallel worlds, dimensions, and levels of space and time.

The more the chakras of your body are purified, the more active are the light chakras above your head. The more life issues you process, purifying the chakras in your system, the better and easier will be your access to worlds where you can literally save humanity. Everything is related to everything else, and everything is connected in a complex way.

While your body is asleep, light work is carried out automatically without you having to concentrate on it. This work is one of the higher goals and tasks of your existence here on this planet Earth at this time. It is happening on the level of your higher consciousness and higher intelligence, to which you are all connected. We are also connected to it.

Your nocturnal journeys, by the way, are one of the reasons why you feel tired or cannot sleep well at this time. This is not only because of the cosmic conditions, the increased Earth frequencies, and the development of your light body but also because of the journeys of your light essence in time and space, which all have an effect on your overall constitution.

Allow yourself as much rest as possible, and spend a lot of time in nature. Do not get confused by the manipulative political information, and stay centered. At this time, the liberation of humanity is imminent—not only on the physical plane but also on the subtle plane—*and this requires the energy, love, and light of each one of you.*

Perhaps, until this moment, you were not aware of the importance of your existence on this planet and at this time. Perhaps you were not aware of the importance of your energy work and your love and light.

Perhaps you have been concentrating mainly on physical help, and you have not been aware of how high and meaningful the task is that your soul and all its parts have undertaken for this incarnation.

We are grateful to you for taking this task upon yourselves. We are grateful that we belong together and support each other. We are grateful for your love, your light, and your willingness to help humanity in its phase of ascension.

The Number Sequence of Remembering

We would now like to give you a new number sequence that will help you live out your radiant core. We call it the "number sequence of remembering." Now is the time in which it is fitting to share this number sequence with you. Step by step, the human community is moving forward, and this number sequence can be shared with you now—at this stage of your evolution, at the proper time.

3 4 3 4 5 7 8 1

This number sequence will help you to more quickly remember the Pleiadian essence within you. It will help you to live out your light-filled and loving task—not only the Pleiadian task but also your human task. It will help you live out your earthly as well as your higher purpose and intention. It will help you to activate and strengthen your healing abilities—not only the Pleiadian ones but also your original essential abilities with which you came to this planet.

Each one of you is different, and each one of you has your own experiences and abilities. This number sequence not only deepens your healing abilities but also connects you to your potentials and your divine abilities. *With its help you will take one more step toward your divine being and your divine light.*

This number sequence makes it easier for you to remember why you came to this planet.

It will help you meet people who will support you as you move forward. Perhaps those of you who meet each other will support each other.

This number sequence connects you with each other through light-filled means.

With light as your basis, you will be better able to connect with each other, enabling you to help other people and the human community. The beautiful, white light of your soul will radiate widely when your mind remembers its task and what is essential for your existence.

Thanks to this number sequence, you will be more visible to the beings of the light world and those human beings that have already remembered the light in their soul. You may find yourself meeting people who oscillate at the same vibration of light as you. You will be given the possibility to attract each other through light-filled means, to meet each other and create new systems, for example, that will also serve others of the human community.

This number sequence protects the light of your soul and the light of your soul essence. The sum of the digits is 8—the infinity and eternity of the light and love of your soul, connection with Divine Intelligence.

You can also program water with this number sequence. Place a glass of water on this number sequence, and allow it to work for at least three minutes. Afterwards, you can drink the water in sips, as needed. You can also place the number sequence near you, carry it with you, look at it, or say it out loud. If you like, you can place it over your heart. Act intuitively.

Peace be with you.
Peace be with us.

18

Telepathy and Creativity Return

The greatest desire we have for this time is to see you and the human community filled with joy. I am sure you can understand this desire, because just as you experience joy when you contact us, so does your joy bring us joy. You can understand it because just as you experience joy and happiness when you remember more and more about your inner self, so does this give us a beautiful feeling of happiness. Everything is connected in this way.

Step by step, you are approaching your true nature. Step by step, you are remembering. Step by step, you are also approaching each other in terms of frequency.

Step by step, the levels of your perception of yourself are being further illuminated, even though the mass media are supposedly in control.

Step by step, your soul and psyche are remembering.

This development and gradual progress are indispensable. Without it, it would not be possible to experience the evolution of the human community. Step by step, you are moving toward the light and toward those levels where love reigns. Not everyone has chosen this development, which should be accepted.

Your mind and thinking—in fact, your entire psyche, which has been manipulated until now—is expanding its horizons and entering spaces and times that were hidden before, hidden and withheld. Your mind is now entering dimensions it finds interesting, fascinating, essential, and surprising, as well as filled with variety and vibrancy.

Your mind has suffered greatly from manipulation but can finally grow into its greatness and show its expansiveness, beauty, and abilities. Your mind is connecting to those fields of your knowledge that it did not have complete access to in earlier times. Your mind is developing its intuition again and connecting more and more with the intuition of your entire individuality.

The spaces your psyche is now entering are beautiful, colorful, and magical, and doors are opening, one after another, revealing treasures and gems. Until this time, your mind had no access to those spaces, and your psyche felt sad and empty as you ran up against locked doors, day after day, making things difficult for you. Your mind then closed itself off inside you, knowing that another day was not going to bring much positive change.

The spaces your mind can now enter have been created as a result of the transformation of low-vibrational frequencies and dimensions of the energy levels of your planet. Due to the transformation of these dark levels, your mind can now look around at spaces it has always wanted to enter—spaces of fantasy, magic, and adventure; spaces of infinite possibility.

Those of you who are evolving spiritually and consciously and who remember your divine light, at least partially, will affirm that your mind, psyche, and thinking have taken on different frequencies—a different speed and a different perception. Your ability to mentally grasp in its entirety the situation that exists at the moment will speed up and become easier.

You will be able to verify that your mind and thinking are able to connect instantly with the mind of another person and perceive, assess, and feel the thoughts of that person more quickly, even instantly.

Your soul will help your mind to do this.

The frequencies associated with the manipulative elements that have influenced your perception are gradually leaving your reality, and as a result, your mind will be liberated. As your freedom increases, you will feel things more than before. Thoughts and ideas will come to you as if out of the blue, because your mind will be able to visit the spaces of imagination and all possibilities whenever it wants to. The ideas that come to you will bring you a creativity you may have forgotten.

Each and every one of you is creative, and each and every one of you carries potential within you. Each and every one of you is different, unique, and each and every one of you is original.

Your mind will be able to connect with several people at once and read their thoughts with purest intent. It will be capable of telepathy, and that is another step toward peace.

Telepathic perception will spare you humans many misunderstandings and mistakes. You will perceive how the other person is feeling and what is going through their mind. You will understand each other better without words. This will enable you to avoid unnecessary situations that bring discord and stress.

Maybe some of you have already felt this new power and ability that your mind makes available to you. Maybe you have found that thoughts, ideas, and creativity have been coming to you in ways you have never experienced before but feel good. You feel that you are re-finding yourselves, your essence.

How quickly you reach your essence is not important. The important thing is that you are already on your way. The important thing is that you have already set off. Your life story so far, or what kind of person you were, is of no matter. The important thing is that you have set out on this path and chosen self-knowledge. Your path is your destination. Your path is the essential thing, the most important thing, the thing you must never forget on your path. It is the purity of your heart and your actions. You may make mistakes along the way. You may be subject to errors and misunderstandings. But that is part of this path. That is part of it, and that is what enables you to grow.

Your path is your goal in life, the goal for this incarnation you are experiencing. It was already the goal in past incarnations as well, but perhaps you have now realized that you had forgotten this fact in your past incarnations or that you were prevented from recognizing it.

You have been living beneath the veil of forgetting in a state of forgetfulness, unable to connect with your heart, your soul, your mind, or your body. You lived, but your existence felt like it meant nothing.

At this time, it is possible for you to experience your incarnation as you imagined it would be, and as you planned it for yourself in the world of light. The cosmic conditions bear witness to this.

For many of you, the incarnation you are going through now is the most important of all.

For many of you, it is the last, final incarnation on this planet. Perhaps you have reached the goal of your journey?

For many of you, it is clear that you want to live through further incarnations on this planet. You want to experience the abilities you have now recovered.

It does not matter which option you choose. It does not matter what decision you made or will make. It does not matter how many more incarnations on Earth you choose to live through.

The important thing is to live every day of your existence to the fullest, no matter the form, dimension, or planet. The important thing is to live every moment of being with purity in your heart and mind and joy of the moment, being in the moment of daily life.

Look at the world around you, which is manifold and wonderful. You will see and feel the diversity and splendor, if you wish to see it and feel it. It is up to you whether you choose this option.

Your mind, soul, and light beings connect you to whatever you wish to concern yourselves with and to the world you choose to live in. We wish with all our hearts for you to choose a world that is manifold and wonderful. We have also chosen this option; we have chosen multiplicity and magnificent beauty.

We are with you. We love you. We accompany you in every step of your existence.

Peace be with you.
Peace be with us.

PART TWO

Messages from the Pleiadians for the New Era

19

You Are Entering the New Era

First message from the Pleiadians about the New Era

channeled on 19 January 2021

Dear people of Earth!

Every second of your space and time and heightened cosmic frequencies is reaching your planet Earth. These light frequencies illuminate the systems of all human beings who open themselves and are ready for their consciousness development.

These cosmic light frequencies also illuminate every corner of this planet. Dark beings and dark elements are experiencing difficult situations and difficult times.

The time of the dark beings and dark elements on this planet will soon be over.

The light that is coming to Earth cannot be ignored.

Every day, thousands of people are awakening, and their hearts are connecting with each other through the power of light and love. Every day, the light of human hearts, which is key to spreading radiant, divine power on this planet—increases. Every day on this planet, children are born that carry divine love and heightened cosmic consciousness.

Every child that arrives brings with them a part of their heightened consciousness and a part of the consciousness of the Divine Source. Every child that arrives increases the energy and light of their earthly family and environment. Every child that comes to you and every child that lives on this planet is a gift from God. You are entering a new age, new light-filled levels, and a new future. You are entering new frequencies and previously unknown levels of consciousness within this body. The light revolution is transforming the old systems into new structures. You are at the beginning of an upheaval of those systems that have served the dark forces for millennia!

You are at the beginning of a New Era that will bring even more light to this planet. Every day, bubbles of truth come to the surface. Every day, with increasing frequency, the truth flashes forth through the minds of human beings.

This is not an easy process but, over time, it will bring success and peace to human beings.

Please do not forget that the destructive systems on this planet have endured for millennia. It is not possible to change everything that exists within a few months. It is a process that requires your increased trust, as well as increased light from your heart organs. Every one of you is also in a process of your own. Every one of you has voluntarily chosen this process in the heaven of human beings.

Every one of you is going through the greatest, most important, and most advanced process of all your incarnations on this planet so far. Every one of you is involved in your own personal process and at the same time in the overall process. Every one of you influences the overall process, and every one of you carries a part of the future of humanity in your hands.

The Great Change will come when you have changed yourself and found your essence and the great light within you. You are the change! Please do not forget this fact. Every one of you is important. Every one of you is magnificent.

Do not wait for the change "out there." Start changing your personal system for the better. Your illuminated system connects with the illuminated systems of other people.

⌒

Go out into nature often, and start meditating for at least a few minutes a day. Through meditation, the systems of your mind, soul, and body unite into one, and your heart, at the moment of unification, is able to receive cosmic light and distribute it throughout your system.

In this way, you will become a huge cosmic light on this planet. Through meditation, your intuition increases. Your intuition lets you know which decisions for the future are right for you. Through intuition, you can choose the people with whom you want to continue on your earthly path.

Live to the best of your potential. Do what you do best. Your potential is a quality that draws more light and more life energy into your life. Find what you do best and what distinguishes you.

Through this, you connect with the morphogenetic fields of your own power and your own energy!

Although it may seem to many of you that the situation on this planet is disadvantageous, when we look ahead into your human future, we see that the future of humanity will be light-filled, harmonious, and peaceful.

The timeline of human development is spiraling, and the direction forms a positive line, even if this line is obscured by the frightening news of the media. The news of the media has frightened your soul and mind, and partially disconnected you from your natural intuition. Please realize that this belongs to the plans of the dark forces.

Please also be aware that the light and love found in human hearts are stronger than the dark, destructive elements. Do not forget that each one of you originated in the light and come from the Divine Source.

Realize that, sooner or later, love and light will spread out completely over this planet and that everything dark existing here will undergo divine correction.

Persevere in your positive and light-filled actions. Stay in your power and personal and holistic process. Only then can you spread your light.

We thank you for your courage and for being here on this planet.

We thank you for your perseverance and determination.

We thank you for the fact that your soul is in a human body right now.

We thank you for helping the overall development and light-filled evolution of humanity through your incarnation on this planet.

We are incredibly proud of each and every one of you. Through your incarnation here on Earth, you are also helping the members of your family who are currently in the heaven of human beings. You are helping the healing of your family as a whole.

We wish you much strength for this year.

This year will be full of light from a cosmic point of view. From a human perspective, it will be revolutionary—revolutionary in terms of consciousness.

We will always be here to support you on the energetic level if you ask us for help. We are with you and look forward to the increased light that will be shining this year, which connects us with you through light-filled means.

We look forward to being close to you.

This year will be magical.

*We wish you much happiness
and peace in your hearts.*

Your Pleiadian Companions

20

Choose Light-Filled Transformation for Yourself

Second message from the Pleiadians about the New Era

channeled on 13 March 2021

Dear Messengers of Light on planet Earth!

Day by day the influx of cosmic light is increasing, raising your light and the light of your earthly plane.

Day by day, the light in your soul is also increasing. Your soul light transmits this light to the systems of your personal existence, the personal existence of each and every one of you.

In these weeks, the gates to the light-filled dimensions of the new level of consciousness are opening very quickly. The many years of preparation that have taken place since 2012 on the energetic level are now bearing fruit in the form of increased cosmic frequencies and information that your planet is successfully encoding in itself.

Your planet also encodes this cosmic light information in the souls of human beings, if they are ready for it and open to it. The upheaval of consciousness that is taking place is a natural development of the human community. Individuals who think and act in dark ways are instrumental in opening the eyes and broadening the horizons of thousands of human beings every day with their negative standpoint. These darkly thinking and acting individuals have taken this heavy task upon themselves in order to help thousands of human beings to awaken more quickly from their long sleep. Life on planet Earth is, in a sense, a game, and each one of you physically alive on this planet right now is playing an important role in the overall development of the human community.

Every earthly incarnation of a human being at this time serves the process of awakening and the processing of personal issues so that humanity as a whole can successfully ascend into the higher dimensions of consciousness.

Every one of you plays a major role in this comprehensive shift toward the light.

Everyone who has decided to increase their personal light and enter into higher dimensions of consciousness has been provided with a greater number of light beings from the light world that support them and bring them new, increased cosmic light frequencies.

At this time, every one of you, without exception, has been given their own personal portal of light to the fifth dimension of consciousness by the spiritual world. Nearly eight billion people living on this planet have received their own portal of light, which is situated above each one of them, directly above each one of you.

The purity of your heart, a pure intention, and the decision to ascend into this new dimension of consciousness connect you to your personal light-filled level of consciousness. This pillar of light is approaching you steadily, and the purest essence of your soul connects you with it. The light of this portal connects you with other pure-hearted human beings who have made the same choice as you.

It is enough to choose this opportunity to ascend, and it is enough to realize that the purity of your own heart is the access code to these new light-filled dimensions.

Every human being, without exception, now has the opportunity to choose this new dimension. But not all human beings will ascend to this light-filled level, because their consciousness and spiritual development will not allow it. Nevertheless, these human beings will benefit from the heightened cosmic frequencies of consciousness, and their decision will be respected by Divine Intelligence. Everyone has free will, and everyone has the right to their own personal free choice. Everyone has the right to bear the consequences of their own decisions.

Many of you have been waiting a long time for this time of light-filled change. Many of you are feeling the heightened cosmic frequencies. You feel it not only physically but also in your soul. Everyone who commits themselves to their continued spiritual development will find that this happens much faster than before. The cosmic light frequencies and light information will help you. The increased number of personal light companions will also help you in your development. What matters, as always, is your intention.

Integrate the cosmic light frequencies of the new levels of consciousness into your heart every day.

Purify your body, soul, and mind every day with metallic gold color, which has the ability to rewrite and reprogram any burdensome programs in your systems through light-filled means.

Purify your aura with violet transforming light, and let all the elements that have polluted your aura be transformed in this light. Connect every day with Earth, which carries heightened cosmic frequencies. You will feel her power and wisdom.

Stay connected to your power, energy, and confidence in this way. Stay in your positive intention to make your own decisions about your health—to decide IN FAVOR OF the health of your body and IN FAVOR OF the health of your soul.

∽

Do not forget that truth, divine truth, is an immeasurably great, independent power that comes directly from the Divine Source. Truth has such tremendous power within it that, sooner or later, it will always come to the surface. It is so strong that it is not possible to hide it for any length of time or to keep it from people by hiding it under the surface of knowledge and events.

Do not forget that a lie, no matter what kind, has no inherent power of its own. It must be constantly nourished and fed artificially in order to survive and exist. A lie does not come from the Divine Source and does not carry divine power. A lie can be used for a certain time but also tends to transform its vibration into light.

On this planet there will only be amplified cosmic light in the future—not only within the earth but also within the souls of the inhabitants of this planet. There will no longer be any room for dark elements, lies, or negative actions among you.

Light and divine love will fill all the corners and spaces of this divine planet.

Affirmation for the Absorption of These Light Frequencies into Your System

Breathe deeply in and out. Place your hands on your heart.

Now say aloud:

"Now and in this space, I receive the light frequencies of my positive future.

Now and in this space, I integrate the light frequencies of my positive future into my entire system.

Time and space are one.

My light beings accompany and protect me.

I bless my future.

I bless my life.

I bless myself.

I bless my light beings.

Thank you, thank you, thank you."

Feel your heart accepting these divine gifts and your body increasing its light-filled energy.

Breathe deeply in and out, and be aware of your heightened spiritual awareness, which connects you to further light-filled spaces and times in your existence.

We thank you for your light work.

We thank you for being.

We thank you for existing.

> *Peace be with you.*
> *Peace be with us.*
> *Your Pleiadian Companions*

21

We Are Transmitting Increased Light & Love to You

Third message from the Pleiadians about the New Era

channeled on 14 June 2021

Dear Messengers of Light!

All of you who are on this planet here and now have chosen to be a part of this great era. You are all a part of this significant event and are carrying out important tasks—tasks that you have set for yourselves for this incarnation.

Events on this planet are picking up speed very quickly. Even if the mass media hide the divine truth, the results of what is happening behind the scenes will change the future of humankind for the better.

Through the words we are addressing to you right now, we wish to give you strength. We wish to give you confidence and perseverance for your positive actions.

Planet Earth very much appreciates positive action because this supports her. Planet Earth is going through truly great changes. Planet Earth has already reached higher dimensions of consciousness and invites every one of you to accompany her on the path of light.

Many of you did not expect Earth to increase her light frequency so quickly—and rest assured, even from a cosmic perspective, it really is happening in an incredibly short time.

Humankind is a visitor to this planet.

And your planet Earth, which is a mother to each one of you, is connected to every one of you in light and frequency. She is connected to you through the strength of her subtle yet powerful energy, which allows you to perceive what life feels like on higher levels to an ever-increasing degree.

Every human being now has the opportunity to purify those personal karmic matters that still need to be processed. And Mother Earth is supporting you all on your earthly path.

Every one of you has chosen this incarnation in this time and space independently and voluntarily—every one of you. You may just not be able to remember that fact.

At the same time, humanity as a whole is currently processing a karmic matter that humanity has decided to successfully complete and transform.

The role that the soul of humanity is playing at this time is essential for each one of you and is in direct communication with the soul of planet Earth. The soul of humanity is a noble, radiant consciousness intelligence, which, through its light, supports each one of you with the light of the Divine Source.

Do not forget that above the level of your human consciousness there are other fields of consciousness that attract you and support you with their light and love.

Remember that you are *not* alone here.

Do not forget that the events required to enable the processing of the karmic affairs of humanity follow a predefined plan.

Everyone who has decided to successfully fulfill the aims of their incarnation will receive support from the light world.

Everyone who, by virtue of their purest intention, has decided to successfully process their karmic affairs has connected themselves with the light-filled levels of space and time in higher dimensions.

∾

As we have said before, we wish to transmit more light and love to you. We wish to transmit light and love to all your systems. This phase you are in right now will ultimately guide you to the state of freedom and peace. Nevertheless, you are now experiencing enormous pressures, which burden you as human beings.

We deeply understand what you are dealing with, for we, too, once found ourselves in an almost identical situation. Our population also suffered from occupation and manipulation by dark forces. We, too, found ourselves in a situation where it seemed like there was no escape. Many of us believed the manipulative words of the dark beings and acquiesced to their shameful deeds. They took a similar path and adopted a similar frequency.

Many of the members of our community embarked on this low-vibrational path because they had forgotten their inner light and connection to the Divine Source. Many of them lost their physical lives. We had to learn to accept and respect that their decision was voluntary. We had to learn that processing karmic matters served our common whole.

A part of the population that had not forgotten the light in its soul began to act more positively. We began doing group meditations. We began mutually connecting the light of our souls with increased intention. We performed global meditations, connecting with the Divine Source and its intelligence. We sent gratitude to the soul of our civilization and the soul of our Pleiadian planets.

Our intention to positively change the situation by light-filled means increased the light frequency of the entire population. Through our light-filled energy work, we also helped those souls that had left their physical bodies. We increased the light of the entire population, healing our karmic affairs as a whole.

Our efforts and our conviction that we wanted to free ourselves from those manipulating beings and powers summoned the help of other cosmic companions. They helped us initially on an energetic level. But after a certain time they were allowed by the Cosmic Council to come down to our planet and help our civilization to build new systems based on divine truth, on divine consciousness, and on the use of cosmic elements, such as free energy or plasma.

The dark beings and powers left our planet when they realized that there was no more room for their dark deeds in our community. We are convinced that your human community will experience a similar sequence of events.

The love and light in your heart is the most important value for your personal and holistic liberation. Every positive thought and emotion purifies and heals the collective field of humanity. Every one of you who connects to the light world is helping others to successfully connect as well.

Every one of you is playing an important role, at this time—a role for your own personal development and for the overall development of humanity. Every connection to the light beings and to the light world illuminates the collective human field of consciousness.

You have already come so far, each and every one of you! Please do not stop now, before the completion of this phase.

The number of angelic beings and light beings close to you is greater than ever before, and these light beings have come to your aid. They came to your aid so that your hearts would remain pure and would not be closed by fear caused by the manipulation being imposed on humanity.

All these light beings have come to planet Earth voluntarily, just as you also came down to this planet voluntarily. Together, you follow an inconceivably great plan. You are in the process of purifying the collective consciousness of humanity and ascending into higher dimensions of consciousness. Through your light work and love, you are helping your children and all further generations of the human civilization to follow.

We would now like to send you some very personal supporting frequencies.

Open your heart and accept our love, our energy, our support, and our light.

Accept the healing frequencies of the cosmos.

Accept the gratitude and love of the Divine Source and all the light beings that are around you.

At this moment, we are all in loving connection and union with you.

Now, now and here.

Time and space are of no consequence.

Breathe deeply and connect to the heightened frequencies of light that are flowing to you right now.

Observe how your heart is shining, full of light, and how it is absorbing all these positive light frequencies.

Your heart is passing on all these positive frequencies to your soul, mind, and body.

Breathe deeply, in and out.

Now, to support this process you can say:

"I accept all these healing frequencies with gratitude.
I am love.
I am light.
I am gratitude.
I am freedom.
I am divine existence.
I am.
Thank you. Thank you. Thank you."

We thank YOU for your energy work and for your unity.

Peace be with you.
Peace be with us.
Your Pleiadian Companions

22

Your Healing and Regeneration through the Grace of God

Fourth message from the Pleiadians about the New Era

channeled on 20 September 2021

Dear Messengers of Light!

We bring you warm greetings from our time–space. We would like to share some information with you concerning the planetary situation.

The hearts of human beings are opening. The current situation entails great purification of the thinking mind and purification of the emotional essence of the human soul. Simultaneously, this global phase is leading to a time in which human beings will gain an overall picture of what is truly fundamental, what is essential, and what deviates from the normal.

Beyond the complexity of the general situation, this time is bringing new perspectives and new opportunities. Through the current challenges, the human minds of many human beings are beginning to connect to the matrix of galactic knowledge and wisdom. The withdrawal of every single human being from the familiarity of previous, entrenched work processes holds the possibility of new perceptions, new thoughts, and the beginning of new community structures.

The human mind and soul does not find it easy to go through this incarnation in a human body. It is not easy to participate, first-hand, in the global situation in a human body. It is not easy to accomplish the tasks that the human soul and spirit have set for themselves in the heavenly heights.

We know that physically experiencing this situation—a kind of learning task for earthly life—feels different from the way the human soul had imagined it would be while in the heavenly heights. At the same time, however, it is a joy for every human soul to be allowed to spread its light over this planet and to fulfill its planned tasks, step by step.

Step by step, human hearts are opening.

Step by step, the levels of the human dimensions of consciousness are being illuminated.

Step by step, human beings are beginning to perceive the current reality as a karmic matter that needs to be healed.

The light of human hearts is changing the whole course of development. The light in your hearts is raising you to higher levels.

Many beings around the world have already liberated their minds and souls. Many beings have freed themselves from manipulation and from the weight of oppression. Many human beings around the world have understood that only through their personal understanding and a personal overview of the overall situation will they be able to free themselves and step out of the existing 3D matrix. They came to this decision themselves; they found their truth themselves, after beginning to understand the situation from a higher perspective. Their purified heart has connected them to the frequency of freedom, truth, and life energy.

Stepping out of the 3D matrix now allows their soul and spirit to vibrate in the luminous 5D frequency, the fifth dimension of consciousness.

It is very important for us to inform you that many millions of people on this planet have already stepped out of the 3D matrix mentally and emotionally. Every day, the numbers are increasing enormously; thousands more are rising above these low vibrations. We want you to be aware of this fact because we know that the mass media are keeping you imprisoned in lies and imprisoned in hopelessness.

The overall condition of the current situation has caused many inhabitants of this planet to wake up. We are aware that a countless number of you feel that the social power game will not change for the better. You feel that there are so very few of you as yet. But exactly the opposite is true! There are already a great many of you! And every day, as we have already told you, more and more people on this planet are waking up, thousands more.

The awakening of each individual is like the birth of a new human being on this planet. That is a fact. And that makes us very happy.

In the hearts of awakened people, there is a light that will be so strong in the near future that it will spread all around the planet. This light from the hearts of awakened people will then transform everything into light that is vibrating at a low level and still hiding on Earth, in every corner and in every place.

At the moment of this transformation, divine light will pass through human hearts. Like a ray or a bolt of lightning from heaven, this divine light will flash through the hearts of human beings. It will be of a certain frequency, a specific vibrational level of divine light that has long been awaited and that will now finally liberate you. There will also be a temporal shift into the original time–space that will separate you from the dark beings.

That it will happen is beyond question. It is only a question of how much time it will take before this particular intensity of light in human hearts is reached, until they connect with each other and trigger a complete transformation of any low-vibrational elements on Earth.

Hold out. Do not give up. You are not alone here.

We know that the manipulation of the dark beings is particularly strong in Europe. But light and love are the most powerful things that exist, and something wonderful is happening at the same time.

Since June 2021, divine healing has been taking place in the human community, both in the physical community and in the non-physical community in the heaven of human beings. It appears as a beautiful light-blue light that heals, and we call it *the Grace of God*. This divine light heals human beings and the souls in the heaven of human beings and releases them from the imprisonment of manipulation, untruth, and collective negative affairs. It heals the human body of genetic stress. It purifies and heals entire systems.

This beautiful, light-blue divine light shines through the systems of human beings and human souls in the heaven of human beings, and at the same time, frees them from the weight of manipulation from the earthly incarnations they have lived through.

Thanks to this beautiful light-blue light, even human DNA is capable of regeneration and healing, because this light contains all the information of the divine light as well as the highest form of healing. Those with a pure heart, a light-filled vibration, and a good-natured mind automatically draw this light into their overall system.

The manipulation of the dark beings has been very strong for a long time—too strong for the human civilization to be able to heal itself from it. Divine Intelligence therefore decided that anyone open to this healing can connect to this divine healing light and be healed.

We know that some people have no idea that they are being healed by Divine Intelligence right now, but they receive this healing nevertheless.

We know that some people do not want to accept this light. This is everyone's personal choice. Everyone must decide this for themselves.

We know that this divine healing is another small part that will contribute to the liberation of the human community— the liberation of the physical community and the non-physical community. Every human being is playing an active or passive role in this global situation. It is of no matter whether it is active or passive; what matters is the overall plan of liberation of the human community.

Every human being has a certain role to play. Every human being has a different personal plan and a different path. But every role and every path leads to the goal of divine perfection and wholeness.

If you wish, you can take this healing divine light into your system now.

It is enough to connect to it mentally.

Let gratitude arise in your heart.

Gratitude brings you into the sacred chamber in the heart of the human being. Gratitude opens that sacred chamber in your heart.

And this space allows you to receive the frequencies of healing and the grace of God into your overall system.

Let your heart radiate and breathe deeply.

Now speak the following affirmation. The vibration of your words will connect you with the frequencies of the cosmos.

Affirmation

"Now and in this space, I connect with the consciousness of my heart and with the consciousness of my heart chakra. I ask them to receive all the healing frequencies of divine healing that come to me.

Now and in this space, I connect with my Higher Self. I ask for its support in my healing.

Now and in this space, I am ready to receive the healing and the grace of God.

I now ask for the healing and regeneration of all the systems of my soul, mind, and body.

I ask for healing and regeneration of my DNA.

Healing and regeneration are happening in the here and now. Time and space are one.

I accept everything with gratitude.

My healing and regeneration bring me divine wholeness and perfection. The purest essence of my soul connects me in the here and now with the purest essence of the Divine Source.

I hereby confirm the healing and regeneration of all my systems.

I bless myself on all levels of my being.

Thank you, thank you, thank you."

Breathe deeply, and take your time to allow all the healing frequencies in your system to take effect and encode.

Peace be with you.
Peace be with us.
Your Pleiadian Companions

23

Your Light Brings Awakening to Others

Fifth message from the Pleiadians about the New Era

channeled on 29 December 2021

Dear Messengers of Light on this planet!

We greet you from the starry heights—from the starry heights that are only a mere thought away from you. We greet you from our light-filled planes and bring you the vibration of the greatest, strongest, and most beautiful feeling there is.

We bring you the vibration of love.

People who have already remembered the light of their inner being are vibrating in the same frequency that we are sending to you right now. The vibration of love makes you realize that love is something that cannot be simulated.

Our love is flowing to you right now, at this moment, and filling your hearts.

People who have already remembered their inner light extend their rays into all levels of their reality. They extend their rays, and also fill with their light the lives of other people, who then also remember, without being aware of it. The light expands, multiplies, and increases its radiant intensity.

Light-filled human beings are already here on this planet in great numbers. Many of these people are just not yet aware that they are part of this group of light-filled human beings. Maybe you also feel that your personal light is not sufficient. Maybe you feel that the light of your soul is not yet radiant enough. But the opposite is the case! Every one of you who, in your thoughts, occupies yourselves with light and love carries light and love within. Every one of you carries your purest essence within you. And your interest in all that has to do with the fact that light and love increases the light and love within you.

Every thought that connects to light and love increases your personal light frequency and light vibration.

Every one of you carries light and love within. Every one of you is important. The light and love within you are important—at this time, they are the most important things you carry within. These two elements are the most important qualities needed to ignite the light of humankind and bring love to the entire planet.

Through your light and love, you heal the whole human community, because you are all connected. Even people who have turned away from you during this time, like you, carry the purest divine essence within them. Every one of you has come from the light. Every one of you carries the radiant essence within you.

Many people have forgotten that, but not you. You continue to follow your goal of soul freedom, thereby kindling the light of your soul more and more.

Your light expands in all directions of your reality. It connects with the purest essence of other human beings. Through this, you are all connected with each other. You are like a living organism—you influence each other.

Your light gives the gift of memory to others. They may not remember right now, they may not remember in the next few weeks or months, but the memory will come eventually. This is what your radiant core wishes. It does not matter how long it takes. Your light brings healing to others. It does not matter in which area their healing occurs. Their system receives your light, nevertheless.

Every moment of your life makes sense from the perspective of higher events and from the perspective of higher consciousness. Every person you meet on this planet influences you in some way, and you influence them. Your meeting, however brief, influences you from a higher perspective for your entire earthly life. Every encounter brings a certain emotion, thought, vibration, frequency, color, or sound. Every encounter influences you and steers you in a certain direction in your life.

The situation that exists on this planet influences all that happens to you as well as the direction of your earthly life journey. This situation gives you new insights and new possibilities. This situation frees you from your entrenched daily rituals and allows you to step onto the path of light to your soul and your existence.

The situation right now brings new opportunities and new ways of life to many more people on this planet.

This situation brings together a great many people of goodwill. Their vibration of love connects their hearts and links their life journeys. Their vibration of heart-love connects them with each other. Do not be concerned that you might miss these people, or overlook them. The love in your heart will show you the right direction. Love unites you and gives you the motivation to create new communities.

New systems are just now emerging. Bring together your powers, your energy, and your abilities, and let new structures emerge that function according to the principles of supreme love. Every one of you holds the future in your hands—not only your own future but also that of humankind. You are connected with each other and influence each other.

Millions of people on this planet have kindled their hearts and are continuing to expand their light. Do not forget that there are many enlightened people living on other continents on this planet as well. And these people who have found their light and liberated the light of their soul also influence you positively.

The light of each one of you is vast and this light unifies through your purest essence.

If you are feeling sad, empty, or hopeless, connect with the purest intentions with people who are already living their personal soul freedom. Connect with their light and with their love. You help each other through this.

Detach yourself regularly from the negative collective field of humanity. Detach yourself consciously, and consciously connect with the positive field of humanity. This positive field grows day by day, increasing its light.

Even if the mass media make you believe in emptiness and hopelessness at every opportunity, the journey to the light is inexorable. The cosmic conditions and the number of enlightened people testify to this. The community of humanity has chosen the path of light and is committed to walking it.

We cannot say how long it will take the human community as a whole to emerge from the dark reality. However, we can say with certainty that the ascent will succeed. Until then, every one of you, as individuals, can step out of the dark reality. Every one of you who decides to step out of the dark reality will be successful.

Millions of people have already stepped out of the dark 3D reality. These are the pioneers who have chosen a bright future. Every one of you has been given this opportunity. Your thoughts connect you with the luminous reality of earthly existence.

Every one of you has the same opportunity. The more of you who step out of the dark reality, the easier it will be for those following you, your earthly successors, to step out of the dark reality. Through your pioneering work, through your positive courage, and through the vibration of love and light in your heart, you create favorable conditions for them on this new path in their earthly reality.

In this way, you help each other.

Do not forget that light multiplies. It spreads out and increases its intensity. Your successors and their successors will find following this path and progressing into the light-filled levels of the positive future easier.

For earthly human beings, the real stepping out of the 3D matrix is beginning at this time. And soon, more people who have chosen to do so will step out of 3D reality, and this will happen much more quickly than you might imagine. You have opened up this path for them, you are the pioneers. You have shown others the way and simplified their path.

In the near future, within the next few weeks and months, millions of people will collectively step out of 3D reality, and this will happen very quickly and easily. One by one, human beings who have chosen a bright future will step out of the low-vibrational levels at an accelerated pace.

The cosmic frequencies, the light beings, your family in the heaven of human beings together with your ancestors, your cosmic family, and the frequencies of the Divine Source all support you and will continue to support you.

At every step, the help of the light world and its light beings is waiting for you.

Do not forget that an innumerable amount of light beings and divine frequencies have been sent to you for the overall transition to light.

Do not forget that many peace-loving extraterrestrial beings are supporting this process behind the scenes of these events and are waiting with you for Divine Intelligence to allow their official arrival on your planet.

Do not forget that many of our Pleiadian companions have descended to this planet and have taken on a human body that will allow them to exist and act on Earth. Many of us are living among you and helping you. I am sure you feel the purity of their soul and behavior.

You are in a phase of transition—of transition into light-filled levels.

Step out of the low-vibrational levels with your thoughts. Step out of those levels, and show others the way. Step out, through the power of your heart vibration, and enable other human beings who do not yet have enough courage or strength to do so to follow your example. Support each other. You are connected. You are a living organism.

Affirmation

If you like, you can support this with an affirmation that we will recite in unison in a moment.

Detach yourself first from everything with a low vibration.

Invite the positive, which will support you and help you on your life journey to soul freedom, into your life.

Connect in thought with your radiant future. Consciously connect with all the light beings that accompany you. Illuminate your heart with love and gratitude.

And now speak the affirmation aloud three times in a row. Your voice connects you to the cosmic, light-filled vibration of these words:

"Now and in this space, I activate the radiant, loving power of my heart.

My heart receives the vibration of light and love.

Through the power of my heart and through the power of my positive thoughts, I connect to the light-filled levels of my being.

The positive power of my thoughts connects me with my positive, radiant future.

Present and future are one.

Space and time are one.

In the here and now, I live the light-filled and loving reality of my being.

I am full of light.

I am loving.

I am perfect.

Thank you, thank you, thank you."

We wish you all much light, love, strength, energy, courage, and trust for the coming year. We are with you. We accompany you, full of light.

With love!
Your Pleiadian Companions

My Epilogue

The New Year has just begun. The festive mood of December is unfolding again in the realms of daily life—this festive mood and the expectation of something great and surprising.

I feel the same in the depths of my soul. Not only do I love the pre-Christmas and Christmas season, I also feel, deep down, that something great and surprising is awaiting all of us, all of us who are ready for it. I feel this more and more every day.

I sense, as do so many other warm-hearted souls, that new spaces and times await us, which we will step into. How much earthly time we will need for this in our human incarnation is of no matter.

What matters is that we step into these spaces.

All the light beings, the Pleiadians, the Earth people, and healers I am in contact with are of the same or similar opinion—namely, that all those who have decided to step into the spaces of the new positive future will step into them. The light beings affirm that the spaces of the positive future have already been prepared and programmed for us by Divine Intelligence.

We all know this, and yet sometimes it is very difficult for us human beings to get through the current time. This path, during this time and in a human body, is not always easy and feels more intense than we had imagined in the heaven of human beings. But we also know that the overall situation is essential to enable us to realize the path to light and freedom.

When we look back, we can see clearly that we have made huge steps in this very short (from a cosmic point of view) period of earthly time—huge steps in our evolution of consciousness, and huge steps toward knowledge of our inner being. These giant steps have moved us onward—*onward to the light.*

We have experienced, and are still experiencing, situations that the Pleiadians made us aware of in advance. In each book in this series, they have consistently given us advice on how best to prepare.

Time after time they told us that our greatest task for this time is to purify our hearts of all emotions of fear. They pointed out to us that in the near future our purified hearts will be the key for receiving and encoding cosmic frequencies of love and light.

They have pointed out to us that a time will come when we must trust our own intuition and not be misled by dark beings, dark powers, and dark-thinking people.

They drew our attention to the fact that it is a pure heart that will liberate us from this overall situation.

We have come a very long way, not only in the present, short, earthly phase—a more than revolutionary time—but also in the time periods of our past earthly incarnations. We have walked together as companions as well as enemies; we have experienced situations that welded us together and those that made us turn away from each other. Everything made sense and follows a higher plan.

We have left many incarnations and many paths behind us. Every path was different and felt different. The only thing that has not changed on the paths of our incarnations is the search for love and light within ourselves and within others.

The search for love and light within ourselves and within others is our inner motor, our inner need. This gives us the strength to go on and enables us to feel more strongly, with each incarnation, *that love and light are our essence.*

In this incarnation that we are in right now, we can finally discover love and light within ourselves and within others. In this incarnation and at this time, we are moving closer to our being and to those things that are essential. The situation "out there" offers us the opportunity to find love and light within.

Not only the whole global situation, but also the cosmic conditions testify to this.

We are in a time of transition—in a time of transition and a change to new times. It is therefore necessary to let go of the "old world"—old energies, old thoughts, and old vibrations.

It is necessary to truly begin anew, and it is best to do so in the way the Pleiadians have repeatedly advised us: We should begin with ourselves, by looking around inside ourselves for those things that no longer serve us and that burden us, looking for what no longer makes sense and what we should discard.

We may have been putting off looking inside ourselves for far too long, knowing that it might be painful and uncomfortable. But when we decide of our own accord to "tidy up" within ourselves, we thereby also "tidy up" the world around us.

Our inner purity will be reflected in the environment and in other human beings and animal beings.

We chose to come to this planet at this time because we knew that this current incarnation was likely to be one of the most important of all time. We have chosen to purify not only our reality but also the reality of humankind.

Our personal purity, love, and light are the driving forces of this time.

The phase we are experiencing right now is an essential period of time that is part of the transition to the new dimensions.

We are not alone in this—and we are not alone *here*. During this phase, the light beings, our light companions, are helping us. And our non-incarnated loved ones permeate our consciousness and bodies and support us in this ascent. They also know that this situation is not easy for us, but they empathize with us. They know what life in the human body feels like.

Our non-incarnated loved ones know that we are more aware of them at this time than ever before. The mental boundaries between the luminous worlds and earthly worlds are beginning to dissolve, and they are able to enter our earthly reality through the power of their love and light. Their radiant, loving power, and guidance are clearly perceptible to us. Our common field of consciousness is becoming more radiant every day, allowing us all to approach the light-filled levels. We are moving forward, hand in hand, and more strongly than ever. We mutually support each other.

~~~~

When I think back to my first contacts with the light world, I remember the first conscious moments I experienced with my non-incarnated family. My family, located in the heaven of human beings, guided me not only into the realms of the heaven of human beings but also into the realms of the cosmic planes and their beings.

I recently went through the "letters" I received from my great-grandfather, who was my first "official" companion in the light world. I received his first light messages many years ago, but reading through them now, I am struck by his incredible wisdom and the parallels that show up in my own life story. Hundreds of light-filled letters that I received from my companions in the heaven of human beings gave us information and hope, and confidence, even then, for the time we are in right now.

One of the letters I received from my great-grandfather I transcribed by means of automatic writing into my computer. You know that I first write all the messages I receive "from above" exclusively by hand, only then do I type them into my PC.

For a long time, I have wanted to share one of his stories with you, because my great-grandfather, together with his wife Leopoldina, was, of my non-incarnated relatives, my first and most important light companion. I am pretty sure he is also connected to the group of Pleiadians that communicates with me.

I never met my great-grandfather in person. He died long before I was born. He was born in 1878 and died in 1957. His story enables you to experience his feelings at least briefly, and it allows you to travel back to a time you may remember from previous incarnations. His tireless search for ways to help others certainly flows through me. My great-grandfather knew even then what the year 2012 would mean for us. He knew about cosmic frequencies already then. He knew about the laws of resonance and about every kind of energetic influence, although he could not have read or informed himself about these things anywhere during the time of his earthly incarnation.

My great-grandfather was connected with the field of knowledge. His constant curiosity connected him to this field.

This light-filled letter, which he transmitted to me from the heavenly heights, was one of his first communications. It was also one of the first light-filled letters I wrote down, back then. Perhaps as you read, you will feel its frequency, its love, and its wisdom.

Basically, my great-grandfather is connected not only with me but also with you. His letter was dictated to me in Old Czech. The words he uses are almost nonexistent in my language. My great-grandfather described his path to the greatest joy of his life on Earth: his path to healing.

I am sure you will receive a great deal of light while reading this wonderful letter, and it is my wish that you will be able to feel the mood of former times held in it.

Hello, my great-granddaughter,

I see you, and I do not know how best to express the happiness this gives me. Every line, every thought of mine that you write down gives me immense joy! My joy is so great that it could probably only be compared to the sun shining brightly and giving people warmth, happiness, joy, and peace. Without the sun, the existence of humankind and all the events and joy here on Earth would not be possible.

I would like to tell you the story of my experiences on this Earth.

When I was a small boy, I also wanted to know and learn about things as much as you do. But at that time it was not possible to learn anything. It was exceedingly complicated to get any information at all from anyone. It was as if I was living among people who did not understand me.

I told my mother and father all manner of things, but they simply did not understand or grasp what I was trying to tell them. They always just said: "Oh dear, our little František is so silly. He is such a dreamer. He talks about human energy all the time, and we have no idea what is going on in his head. He is such an idealist, but he should actually get down to things and do some real work."

But so what?

I carried on going out into nature, and there, there was always something to find out about. The forests around Štikov inspired me so much and, moreover, I found so much wisdom in them. It was absolutely clear to me that birds sing to welcome the new day and bring new beings into the world with their song. It was absolutely clear to me that every process in nature affects us human beings and that everything influences everything else. I studied trees, flowers, grass, animals, and stones, simply everything.

Then, one day, I found a dead squirrel in the forest. I said to it: "If I had come a few minutes earlier, I might still have been able to help you."

It was a complex situation. What would have happened if I hadn't come here at all and hadn't seen the squirrel? Then it would not have affected me. But I had seen it and really wanted to help it with all my might, and I kept thinking about what I could do to help.

Then I asked myself: What if I put my hands on it? I have so much energy in my living body I can share it .

So I put my hands on it. I could feel my hands getting really hot, that is how much I wanted to help the squirrel.

And all of a sudden I felt the squirrel start breathing slowly and moving, then it tried to bite me in self-defense, but by then, I knew I had succeeded. It shook itself and ran away.

That was in 1896, and I was 18 years old. I used to walk around with a little bag of sorts, and that is where I kept the treasures I found along the way. (This little bag is still in the attic at your uncle's, where I was born and where you grew up.)

Then I said to myself that if I could help the squirrel, I could help people. But I did not know how to go about it at that time. I began to play with the idea that there were certain places in every body, centers that provide access for cosmic energy, and not only in a healthy body but also in a sick body.

You know that, in our time, there were no books that could have explained this. Whatever ideas I had came out of my head (now I know that they did not come out of my head, but from other souls that were helping me from above, but back then, I thought that they were my thoughts).

I was looking for these centers in the body so avidly that, at some point, I came up with the idea of looking for them with the help of a divining rod, with which you can find water in a meadow or in the forest. I then successfully managed to determine where these points were. Now I know that these points are "chakras." Back then, however, this was a huge aha! discovery for me. At that time, it was a discovery comparable to the appearance of an airship!

After that, I wanted to know more and more. That is when the first woman contacted me. She was one of the customers for whom our firm had made a prosthetic leg. She kept complaining that her other leg hurt such a lot all the time, and she did not know what she should do. So I used to lay my hands on the leg that was hurting her so badly, and she felt great heat and pain relief each time.

And so we repeated this every time she came to us.

Once a very old man with a very sick heart came. At that time, there were no operations of the kind you know now, and the man had only a few days to live. I maintained that things could not get any worse, and started giving him energy.

The man lived for another 14 years!

And that is how things continued—so many cases and people! But somehow it always exhausted me, which is why I decided I would have to draw energy from somewhere myself, from the cosmos. This turned out to be very easy, because I only had to connect myself mentally to the cosmic energy.

I let myself be nourished by this energy, and I used it to transmit energy to people who needed it and who could not work with it the way I could.

Things went on like that for years, maybe 30 years. In the meantime, I had become a recognized healer and entrepreneur. At that time, entrepreneurs were called "businessmen."

And yet, at some point, from a healing point of view, it was not enough for me. I wanted to do something earth-shattering. So I took a small stick and started looking for water everywhere, and I came across it everywhere.

One day, someone told me there was a very interesting place in the woods near the boggy lakes and meadows near Nová Paka. There was supposed to be an underground spring there that had been proven to be magical. These were just stories, but I began to look into them anyway.

I started going there regularly.

I told myself that the water probably did have healing powers, given all the stories about it, and I decided to do all I could to find out. I actually managed to find the spring, and I began to transport bricks and mortar into the forest so that the spring wells could be lined and serve other people, too.

The water had truly miraculous effects. In addition to the energy I was transmitting to people, I was now also giving them water from the well to drink, and these people magically became healthy straight away.

To this day, I thank all those forces that, through giving me this help, enabled me to become a respected person, both in the neighbor-

hood and far away, which was a very great honor and tribute at that time. I began to study everything I could even more intensively and came to the conclusion that I still knew too little. Everything fascinated me so much that I began to pray to God to allow me to know even more.

All of a sudden, I picked up a piece of paper and a pen and started writing. At first I thought these were my own words and my own thoughts, but that was not the case. I managed to do what you are able to do: I started putting the thoughts of non-incarnated human beings down on paper. This was so incredibly interesting that I experienced feelings of tremendous joy, just like you and others who have this ability. I wrote down the many messages, insights, and healing methods I was allowed to experience, and this gave me great joy.

Unfortunately, a terrible thing happened. All the knowledge I had written down was taken from me by the communists who invaded our house. They took away all the letters I had written with the help of non-incarnated human beings, along with all our money, the vouchers that enabled us to buy food, and all our firm's machines. What I was doing was a threat to them, and I was a dangerous person. The pain I experienced cannot be described. I really wept over that.

But I did not give up, and my contacts with non-incarnated human beings continued. No one could take them away from me.

I carried this knowledge mainly within myself.

We will guard your letters and messages from above, as they will be important for many people on this planet. What you will write down will be incredibly interesting, and it will be used for healing human beings—for healing the mind, the soul, and the body of human beings. It will be for the benefit of humankind.

I can now hand over to you all these many years of work and the things I was allowed to experience in the earthly world and let this information flow through you to Earth.

You see, I no longer need to incarnate. I have decided to help people from above through light-filled means. I did a lot of good during my earthly life, but when I contrast life on Earth with life up here, there is no comparison.

Of course, I also experienced a lot of joy and happiness on Earth, but that cannot compare with the joy and happiness up here. Here, there is so much peace, joy, light, and harmony. Here, we are at peace with all other human souls—also with the communists, who were only sent down to Earth to embody themselves. Now I understand everything.

My dear great-granddaughter, the information we are conveying to you, and will convey to you in the future, will help many people. And the gift I receive for this is that I, together with all the others that convey information, may feel the gratitude of earthly human beings.

A thousand greetings from the light-filled heights!

Your great-grandpa
František Tejnor

I hope you enjoyed his story. I have consciously passed on this letter from him to you. I wanted you all to be able to feel and be aware of the fact that every one of us has healing abilities and a connection to the cosmic world.

Our curiosity and pure intention connect us to these energy fields. Every one of us has access to these fields.

Nothing and no one can stop us in our search for wisdom, truth, love, and the light within us, no matter how drastic and long-term the manipulation on this planet may be.

The manipulation perpetuated by the mass media is an artificial construct that has no power of its own. This construct must be continually fed with lies and further manipulation. We all know in the depths of our souls that the foundations of this construct are now beginning to shake. There are already large cracks in its construction, which will soon cause this construct to collapse.

Until this construct falls entirely, let us be inspired by the wisdom of our ancestors. Let us allow their wisdom, love, and light to flow through us. Let us anchor their wisdom, love, light, and experiences on this planet. Our hearts serve as the key to this.

In the meantime, let us look around at all the positive things that have come into being and see the development of the human mind and its consciousness! Let us observe how fast our minds can think.

Let us observe the resonance in all directions and areas of which it is capable.

Our spirit is just freeing itself from the dark and low-vibrational levels and ascending with us into the spaces of creativity and clarity.

Let us notice the beautiful sunsets that are awaiting us almost every day, illuminating us with their beauty.

Let us observe the beautiful plants in our natural world, and how these plants have linked themselves to their original divine beauty and frequency. Have you also noticed that there are plants in nature that you have never seen before?

Are you also beginning to notice that animals are starting to communicate with us more than before and that we can read their minds?

Just like children who accompany us through our earthly incarnation, they have the ability to communicate with us telepathically and, through their gaze, convey information to our eyes. And do you not find that you can now read other people's thoughts and perceive their emotions more clearly?

Do you not keep finding that your electrical and electronic devices start to malfunction because they cannot withstand the high frequencies of Earth and the high frequencies coming from the cosmos?

Are you also able to observe various flashes or sparks of light with your naked eye that you didn't notice before?

Do you sometimes observe that, in the perception of our earthly time, there are periods in which it feels as if time has expanded?

Does it not also sometimes seem to you that you are only an "observer" of the overall situation and that you do not belong to the lower-vibrational levels of the human community anymore?

Do you also notice that the overall situation has united people of goodwill, giving rise to new ideas, structures, areas of activity, and self-help groups oriented toward the positive future of humanity?

I could name many more phenomena that have begun to emerge during this time.

New communities are emerging at a rapid pace, helping to build a new social structure. At this time, it is essential—more than ever before—to focus on the positive. The positive force and everything that is loving and light-filled has a much greater "mobility" than it had before. If we want to, we can use this enormous magnitude. It is enough to reach out and bring it into your own life. It is enough to integrate it into your own heart.

And our light-filled companions and our Pleiadian companions will certainly support us in this. These light beings have always accompanied us. Maybe we were just not able perceive their light and love at that time. But now, in these momentous times, we can receive and amplify their light and love, by finding light and love in our hearts and living in light and love.

⌒

Dear readers, I now say goodbye to you and send you my gratitude, love, and the light of my heart. I am grateful to each and every one of you.

I wish you a joyful future. I send joy to each of you—joy for your lives and for your families and loved ones.

We are connected in our hearts.

Love and light connect us.

With love!
Pavlina

APPENDICES

Appendix I

Explanation of the Number Sequence
of Remembering – 34345781

This number sequence reminds you of the light of your soul essence. It reminds you of the task with which you came to this planet.

This number sequence activates and strengthens your healing abilities. It amplifies your abilities and divine potentials. It connects you with your abilities and potentials located in the Divine Source and with people who have already remembered the light of their soul essence. It activates the light and the abilities of your Pleiadian soul essence, provided you carry within you the Pleiadian energy and essence. This number sequence protects the light of your soul and the light of your soul essence.

You can also transmit this number sequence to water. Place a glass or jug of water on this, and let it work for at least three minutes. Afterwards you can drink the water in sips, as needed.

You can also place this number sequence near you, carry it with you, look at it, or say it aloud. If you like, place it over your heart. Act intuitively.

343457 81

Appendix II

The Number Sequence with the
Sign of Infinity – 57819

This number sequence will help you neutralize programs, memories, and visions that are burdening you and also, simultaneously, those memories, programs, and visions that have been artificially encoded in your system.

You can also transmit this number sequence to water. Write it down on a white piece of paper using a gold pen. The signs of infinity ensure the continuous working of this number sequence in your system.

Transmit this information to a glass of water for at least three minutes, and drink it in sips as needed. You can drink this programmed water until you feel free from manipulation. You may experience an initial worsening after drinking the programmed water. Act intuitively.

578 | 9 (∞

Appendix III

Identifying Your Life's Mission

Words Transmitted from Archangel Metatron

I heard the words and felt the energy of Archangel Metatron near me, over and over again. I decided to write down his message and make it available to you, dear readers. At this time, his energy is very strengthening for all of us and, I would almost say, essential.

Archangel Metatron is the patron of our planet Earth and the patron of the Akashic Records, in which the records of every one of us are encoded. He cooperates with other archangels, with ascended masters, and with all the radiant beings and cosmic beings that are responsible for planet Earth. He receives instructions from Divine Intelligence and, in this significant time of transition to higher dimensions, he is allowed to neutralize the energy fields and negative records of us human beings in the Akashic Records, provided our heart is already illuminated and we are ready for the neutralization of karmic matters.

In this message he shares with us words concerning our life task here on Earth, as well as a meditation that sounds as beautiful as a fairy tale.

Message from Archangel Metatron

Everyone can receive information from us concerning their life task. Every person who is truly looking for their essence and their task on planet Earth is able to receive the required information.

Be assured that every one of you is capable of connecting with their field of consciousness and receiving answers.

Most of you wonder why you are actually here and why you sometimes do things on planet Earth that are not in accordance with your wellbeing or not what you want to do. You wonder why you are constantly looking for something, and you are aware that you have no idea where you are supposed to be heading and that you never arrive at your destination.

You are on the path of seeking, discovering, and overcoming obstacles.

Every one of you has made a light-filled contract with yourself and with other souls up here, no matter where you live or what nationality you belong to.

Before you came down to planet Earth, you talked to your angels, your non-incarnated relatives, and your light helpers. You discussed and planned when you would come down to Earth, at what moment in time, so that you could work through an issue that was important to you. You coordinated things with other souls with whom you wanted to incarnate together.

You can think of it as a council of radiant beings that meets and discusses all the details of your incarnation. It usually takes a lot of light-filled work to think everything through in detail so that your incarnation really serves to purify and illuminate your soul.

Every human soul knows in advance what its life on Earth will be like.

We understand that it is often incomprehensible to you that someone would plan a life full of suffering and adversity. This all has to do with karmic matters and restoration. Sometimes, it is important for a soul to experience undesirable and unpleasant things first-hand. Every soul can learn from this.

You choose your family, your friends, and relatives. You plan a suitable moment for your birth.

It is by no means optimal to set a fixed date for birth. Many women choose the date on which to give birth via a Caesarian operation or induction, simply because this date suits them or because they do not want to experience birth pains. But by depriving the child of the possibility of a natural birth date, they change their child's destiny and future timeline. Parents then often wonder why their child is unbalanced, restless, and difficult to guide. They deprived their child of the possibility of a natural birth. In most cases, these little human beings are now headed for a life in which they can all too easily lose their way, because they just do not know what to do with it.

But let us return to the subject of the Council of Light before incarnation. The Council of Light approves the lines and trajectories of destiny put forward by the soul. After a while of being in the light, the soul becomes aware of all the bad things it has done in its life on Earth, to itself or others.

Diverse family entanglements are what mostly lead to the mistakes made, and often the whole family incarnates once more so that, in various family constellations, negative actions and patterns can be dissolved. Marital partners regularly incarnate several times on Earth if their marriage keeps exhibiting the same negative patterns. The roles in families or in a partnership are often reversed so that the soul can feel what the others felt in previous incarnations.

The soul and the angels put forward their plan to the Council of Light. The Council of Light consists of highly evolved and pure beings. Their task is to advise and plan new incarnations. They cooperate with the angels of the souls that want to incarnate and with Divine Intelligence, which approves each light-filled contract before the soul descends.

Every soul is given certain life tasks by the Council of Light:

Task 1 *consists of purifying yourself.*

Task 2 *consists of passing on heart love to other human beings and animal beings.*

Task 3 *differs, depending on how much the soul has been illuminated and how much it has learned in its last incarnations on Earth. If it has already reached a high level of illumination and has worked on itself a great deal in past incarnations, it will receive additional tasks, which it will gladly take upon itself. These are human beings who carry within them the desire to help others.*

These souls bring to Earth the unconditional love of Divine Intelligence. They may bring various messages from the light world, for example. They can heal with their will and the power of their illuminated soul. They bring to Earth ideas for the positive development of humankind, the salvation of nature, and so on. Everything positive that serves to help humanity, no matter in what form or to what extent, every form of help and every idea for the benefit of your human community can be included in your third, additional task.

The first task is always your top priority. If you are not pure enough, you are unable to convey unconditional love, because your heart is not sufficiently connected to divine power and is not strong enough to live absolute unconditional love.

You can, however, work on yourselves fruitfully. Look around and see what needs to be changed for the better or who might need help. It may turn out that you have already worked on yourself enough, and your mind will awaken to what your task in life really is.

If you feel that purifying yourself is not the only reason you came here, remember the Council of Light. Your life task is stored in the Akashic Records, and everyone has access to that.

Exercise: Remembering Your Life Task
on Planet Earth

Transmitted by Archangel Metatron

Sit or lie down comfortably and breathe deeply.

Call Archangel Metatron and your light beings to you, and experience, with all your senses, how these light beings are connected with you.

Archangel Metatron is nearby and smiling at you. You feel his love. He is pleased that you wish to recognize the meaning and purpose of your life, and he knows very well that you have already mastered many life tasks and challenges. He understands that it is important to you to move forward with your development. He is pleased that you are working on raising your consciousness.

Reach out to Archangel Metatron, and let him carry you upwards into higher dimensions. With him, you rise higher and higher, and soon you can see your house, its surroundings, and the town where you live, from above. Metatron shows you your family, your relatives, and your friends. You recognize them quite clearly.

Now Archangel Metatron asks you to look at yourself from this height. Observe yourself and your life on planet Earth. Do you have a feeling of happiness or one of uncertainty or embarrassment? Observe, but do not judge or try to correct the situation. Archangel Metatron only wants to show you how you appear to yourself from a higher perspective.

Archangel Metatron takes you by the hand.

You both soar even higher and leave your life on planet Earth behind. You continue to rise together and pass through different colorful dimensions of the universe, pulsating with life.

Azure blue surrounds you, the color of your sky. Now the golden color of your sun unites with you. You climb even higher, and the golden color mixes with a clear, sparkling silvery color. Here, there is absolute silence, and the unconditional love of Divine Intelligence envelops you.

Archangel Metatron guides you farther. He enables you to return to the moment when you drew up your light-filled contract. You experience how your angels and light helpers hover around you and allow you to look at a contract. It is your life task contract for planet Earth. They carry it in their hands, like a precious artifact and lay it on your heart.

Observe the thoughts, feelings, or visions that come to you.

Your first thoughts, your first feelings, your first visions are right, intuitive.

Take your time and experience this magical moment.

Thank everyone who helped you look into your life plan.

Thank them from the bottom of your heart.

If you feel that you have not received relevant information, ask Archangel Metatron to give you enough signs relating to your life task in the next few moments or in the next few days.

Archangel Metatron takes you by the hand, and you descend together. You leave the dimension of silver-gold light and pass through the dimension of the azure color of your sky on your way to the golden color of your sun. He accompanies you back to the spaces of your reality and lets you rest there for a few moments.

Archangel Metatron thanks you for your willingness and desire to follow the task you planned. He bids you goodbye, warmly.

Give thanks for everything.

Breathe deeply and return to this space.

Archangel Metatron,
Patron of the Akashic Records

Bonus Meditation

For All Children on Planet Earth

Connect wholeheartedly with the angelic beings that are responsible for human children. Your intention is sufficient.

Connect with Archangel Metatron. Connect with Archangel Gabriel. Both archangels are patron saints of children.

Connect with Archangel Raphael, who will help you to heal the children you have in mind.

And now speak aloud or in your mind:

"I call all light beings to me and ask them with all my heart to support me in my energy work.

I ask for help for all those children who have left this planet prematurely. Please purify the souls of these children of their past and heal their memories.

Illuminate their past with divine light.

I ask for help for all the children who live on this planet.

Please purify every child of its difficult past.

Purify and heal all these children's systems.

Let the burdens and programs they carry, on account of their families and on account of the past generations of their families, dissolve in divine light.

Illuminate their small bodies, their souls, and their minds with divine light.

Illuminate their past with divine light.

Illuminate their present. Illuminate their future.

And I ask for help for all those children who are still to incarnate on this planet.

Purify their past, heal their memories.
Illuminate their souls with divine light.
Illuminate their future on this planet with divine light.
Thank you, thank you, thank you.
I bless all the children of this planet.
I bless the souls of all the children who have left this planet.
I bless the souls of all the children who are preparing right now
for their incarnation.
I bless their past, I bless their present, I bless their future.
I bless their existence.
Thank you, thank you, thank you."

We thank you all for this energy work and energetic support. Every positive effort heals the whole morphogenetic field of your children—those who are not incarnated at present, the living, and all your future children.

Acknowledgments

Thank you all, dear readers, for your love and trust, which I appreciate very much. Your loving support gives me the strength and motivation to connect on an almost daily basis with the Pleiadians and the light-filled beings and to receive their messages.

I feel your continued connection. Thanks to the messages of the Pleiadians, we have created a common field of light that continues to grow. And every one of you carries a part of this field in your heart and in your life.

Through this connection and this light work, we are healing the common collective field of humanity. In these momentous times, healing this energy field is one of the most important and essential building blocks. Thank you for your light and for your light work.

I would also like to thank all those who participated in the creation of this book. I thank my daughter Nicole for the excellent German translation of the book texts and Hilary Snellgrove for the great adaptation into English. All of the texts contain the same frequency in English and German as in my native Czech.

I thank my publisher, Michael Nagula, his companion in life, and the entire team that gave physical form to the messages of the Pleiadians. Thank you for your wonderful and tireless work.

I thank all my loved ones, who motivated me once again and stood by me.

I thank all the light beings that have transmitted this important and loving information to me.

I wish you, dear readers, much love and light for your future. Each and every one of you is important, every one.

With peace in our hearts!
Your Pavlina

About Pavlina Klemm

Photo by Melanie Daoud

PAVLINA KLEMM was born in the Czech Republic in the Giant Mountains. At the age of 19, she came to Munich, where she still lives and works today. Even as a small child, she had contact with the light world, and as a young adult, the direction in which her life's journey would take her became absolutely clear.

In 1999, shortly before the turning point of time, Pavlina began working intensively with alternative healing methods. Working with healing universal energy not only developed her healing abilities but also increased her connection to the light world and the angelic realm.

Thanks to this connection, she now sees it as her greatest task to convey information concerning universal laws and cosmic developments. Her channeling contacts with the Pleiadian civilization has resulted in many books, CDs, and a card deck, published in

German and other languages, including the English edition of *Light Messages from the Pleiades* (Findhorn Press).

In her seminars, Pavlina caringly accompanies all participants in the spiritual development of their personality and trains them in Pleiadian healing techniques. She not only uses her skills as Lebens-Energie-Beraterin® (Life Energy Counselor) from her Körbler training and as a Reconnective Healing® Practitioner from her training with Eric Pearl, but also her training by Andrew Blake in quantum healing, her training as a medium of the spiritual world by Doreen Virtue, and her training in Russian healing techniques.

Pavlina continues to devote herself to writing about spiritual cosmic laws, their complexity, and their direct influence on our human society, because as she says: "The teaching and recognition of universal laws is as infinite as the universe itself. It brings joy, awareness, peace, and purity to the heart."

For more information and current channelings visit:

https://pavlina-klemm.com

Also by Pavlina Klemm

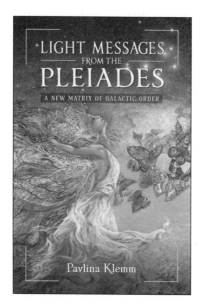

Light Messages from the Pleiades
A New Matrix of Galactic Order

by Pavlina Klemm

*Pleiadian healing techniques to assist humanity
in the ascension process.*

IN THIS HIGH-VIBRATION BOOK, Pavlina Klemm shares
the light messages she has received from the higher beings known
as the Pleiadians on the Great Awakening that is taking place
worldwide. Included are exercises, affirmations, and meditations,
all charged by the Pleiadians with positive frequencies that activate
remembering and healing.

978-1-64411-825-2

FINDHORN PRESS

Life-Changing Books

Learn more about us and our books at

www.findhornpress.com

For information on the Findhorn Foundation:

www.findhorn.org